Speak Truth to Power

Speak Truth to Power

The Story of Charles Patrick, a Civil Rights Pioneer

MIGNETTE Y. PATRICK DORSEY

THE UNIVERSITY OF ALABAMA PRESS
Tuscaloosa

Copyright © 2010
The University of Alabama Press
Tuscaloosa, Alabama 35487-0380
All rights reserved
Manufactured in the United States of America

Typeface: AGaramond

Cover photo courtesy of Charles and Rutha Patrick's family album.

∞

The paper on which this book is printed meets the minimum requirements of American
National Standard for Information Sciences—Permanence of Paper for Printed Library
Materials, ANSI Z39.48-1984.

Library of Congress Cataloging-in-Publication Data

Dorsey, Mignette Y. Patrick.
Speak truth to power : the story of Charles Patrick, a civil rights pioneer / Mignette Y.
Patrick Dorsey.
p.   cm.
"Fire Ant books."
Includes bibliographical references and index.
ISBN 978-0-8173-5556-2 (pbk. : alk. paper) — ISBN 978-0-8173-8266-7 (electronic)
1. Patrick, Charles, 1918– 2. African Americans—Civil rights—Alabama—
Birmingham—History—20th century. 3. African Americans—Alabama—
Birmingham—Biography. 4. Birmingham (Ala.)—Race relations. 5. Birmingham
(Ala.)—Biography. I. Title.
F334.B69N434 2010
323.1196'0730761781—dc22
                                                              2009049901

For
Dad and Mom,
who endured
and
lived to speak
the truth

And ye shall know the truth,
And the truth
Shall make you free.
—John 8:32

Contents

Preface

I remember newspaper clippings, dozens of them, tattered, worn and yellow. I remember old *Jet* magazines peppered with smooth-skinned brown women all kept in an oversized black scrapbook. The dates were from the 1950s.

Forty years later as a working journalist at the now defunct *Houston Post,* mental images of those clippings resurfaced. I recalled a heroic deed attributed to my father, Charles Patrick.

A visit to Birmingham, Alabama, to see my parents in the early 1990s was a reunion with the ancient scrapbook that had robbed me of my peace, unveiling an area of my subconscious long suppressed.

"Memoirs of Charles Patrick" was falling apart by then, but the articles inside told of a groundbreaking incident that preceded both Rosa Parks's defiant stand and the civil rights movement that followed.

My mother managed to save many of the articles, except one my father insisted existed: a picture of him that ran on the front page of either the *Birmingham News* or *Post-Herald* newspaper in December 1954.

Impossible. White-owned newspapers did not run pictures of black men back then unless the news was negative. Nevertheless, I trekked to the Birmingham Public Library with my sister, Ramona, to scour microfiche.

Hours later, I saw a headline that read: "Says he's willing—Lie test set for man in traffic wrangle." Along with the front-page story was indeed a picture of my father at thirty-six. The date was December 31, 1954. I photocopied it and brought the treasure home. Smiling, Dad stared at his picture, eyes glistening.

In 1997, I took my then fiancé, Joseph, to Birmingham to meet the parents. My mother thought it time to expose me to a life I had never known growing up in Los Angeles. So off to the Birmingham Civil Rights Institute we went for a glimpse of pre-1970s reality.

Segregation is eerie. We saw replicas of shotgun houses, buses and signs that read WHITES ONLY. I saw the word "Colored" plastered on signage. I heard taunting voices in Southern accents spewing racial slurs and insults from hidden speakers. Near the end of the exhibit was a wall that displayed historical highlights, along with recognizable names from the era.

Surprisingly, I saw no civil rights–related events prior to the Rosa Parks's 1955 incident.

No one knew. Birmingham had forgotten Charles Patrick.

As a reporter, I felt compelled to tell the story. As his daughter, I felt compelled to correct the omission. It was not an easy task.

Ask my father to replay a conversation held five minutes ago and he might question to whom he was speaking. Ask him about something that happened fifty years ago, and he can narrate with clarity and crisp recall. Or, at least that was true in the beginning.

Our interviews began when he was eighty-three and spanned seven years from 2002 to 2009. Toward the end, his memory waned, like water slowly evaporating.

When Dad was in the mood for an interview, he would sit still for long periods. Once he was weary of questions, he would repeat himself, raise his voice or abruptly indicate he was through talking.

One year, I interviewed him prior to my sister's graduation in Los Angeles. After he became tired, he began loudly reading and rereading one of the old scrapbook articles about himself. Then he just stopped and stared at me. I got the message.

Later at a nephew's Houston graduation, I fired questions and scribbled notes as youths accepted diplomas and parents cried. He finally grew annoyed. In an elevated tone, he asked whether I had all that was needed to write the book.

On another occasion in Birmingham, he told me, "I've talked to you enough about this; everything you need to know is in the newspapers." He directed me to the articles in the old scrapbook. I left him alone for months.

Black men in the South were regularly beaten by police in the 1950s. What made my father's case unprecedented was that he publicly accused the officers in court. Even more unusual was the shrill outcry of civic support that followed, the outcry of a racially divided community for once singing the same chorus—in 1954!

Armed at first with one white attorney, he aggressively pursued the officers in court, and then watched as unrelenting news articles spanning nearly eight months captured everything. The coverage included editorials, commentaries and citizen letters. The Associated Press disseminated the story via its newswire. *Jet* magazine, the *Chicago Defender, Atlanta Daily World* and *Selma Times-Journal* published news articles. The story went national.

Spurred and obsessed by the desire to clear his name, Dad submitted to a lie detector test without even knowing what it was, and before such tests were widely embraced. As white citizens wrote letters to politicians seeking justice "in the regrettable case of the Negro prisoner who was beaten in jail."[1] As the NAACP gathered at the historic Sixteenth Street Baptist Church (the same church where a 1963 bomb shredded four little girls) to draft resolutions and raise money on his behalf. As a soft-spoken wife encouraged her husband to tell the truth, affording support he needed to withstand.

This book is not only a tribute to my father, but also to the courageous journalists, attorneys, civil rights activists and ordinary citizens of Birmingham, both black and white, who kept his case before the collective conscience of a corrupt and racist power structure.

In 1954, history witnessed the power of the press, the power of black and white citizens, demanding justice. Most important, history witnessed the power of one who, spurred by simple mores and a passion for justice, insisted on right, at a time when much was wrong.

Charles Patrick's story is part of the civil rights story and served as an early foundation for the movement that ensued. His highly publicized and epic fight led to a successful struggle against a brutal, corrupt system in Birmingham, Alabama, in 1954.

And to think it all started over a parking space.

Mignette Yvonne Patrick Dorsey

Acknowledgments

My highest thanks to Jesus Christ, my God and Savior, who kept me going during the research and writing of this project, which spanned more than fifteen years.

My husband, Joseph Paul—who tolerated the writer's moods, cooked, shopped and kept the household going—is priceless. This book is a testament to his love and patience.

I am indebted to my ninety-one-year-old father, Charles Patrick, for facing the worst and living to tell it. His brave stand was monumental, his story, timeless. Having outlived nearly all the key participants in his harrowing saga, he endured years of questions and answered kindly, always checking to see if I had all that was needed after each interview session.

Thanks to my mother, Rutha Patrick, for sticking it out with Dad for sixty-three years, for preserving all those articles from fifty-five years ago, for clarifying key points that were fuzzy for Dad. She was the official fact verifier, who never ventured into court with him, yet encouraged him to speak truth to power. She is the reason.

The support, nourishment, insight and feedback of my siblings and extended family were invaluable. Eternal appreciation for Charles, Christine, Larry, Gregg, Marydeane, Ramona, JoAnne and Freddie for their prayers.

Never-ending thanks to the staff at The University of Alabama Press for their guidance, understanding, patience and flexibility. I am also grateful for the invisible reviewers who offered tough critiques that made me tighten, edit, revise—delete, delete!

Thanks to Daniel Sanders, who advised and oversaw contract matters. Attorneys Maureen Doherty and Al Staehely also offered valuable legal counsel.

James "Jim" Baggett and his capable staff at the Birmingham Public Library Archives Department offered priceless research assistance that made this book possible; and much appreciation for Brandon Crawford Smith in the Microfilm Department for his vast knowledge and expertise.

I am grateful for attorney M. Wayne Wheeler, Principal Magistrate Peter Hall Jr., Virginia Van der Veer Hamilton, and James A. Robey Jr. They were generous and forthcoming with information about their fathers, who, of course, contributed to my father's exoneration. What their fathers did for mine enabled Dad to live to tell his story.

Highest appreciation for Howell Raines, Rebecca Wheeler, Joe Dickson, Dr. Robert Jensen, Andrew Glaze, the late Wendell Givens, Mason Davis, Arthur Walton, Fred Shuttlesworth and *Birmingham News* editor Tom Scarritt, all of whom fielded questions or offered historical insights.

For the interviews and research assistance, thanks to Dr. Horace Huntley and Wayne Coleman at the Birmingham Civil Rights Institute. Much appreciation to Barbara Shores for providing contact names. I also appreciate Willie Maryland at the Alabama Department of Archives and History and Ted Murphy at Boston University's Martin Luther King Jr. Archive for quick responses to questions.

My gratitude to Everett Gorel at South Coast Film and Video for the gracious way he interviewed my father, for the film footage and for helping clarify the vision. I am grateful to Yoruba Richen for sharpening that vision.

Thanks to Deborah Mann Lake and the late Judy Lunn, writers extraordinaire and friends, who first shared the excitement about my father's story in the *Houston Post* newsroom one day. I only wish Judy, who chided me for not having commenced on this book sooner, had lived to see its completion.

To everyone unnamed who prayed, advised, corrected, rebuked, guided—thank you.

Speak Truth to Power

I

A *Nigger* Defined

I learned my father's definition of *nigger* during a game of dominoes in the 1980s. Bones slamming, insults flying and me losing. The permanent crease between Dad's eyebrows deepened as he contemplated strategies. It was tough beating him. Still is.

Suddenly, the telephone rang. Mom answered. It was an in-law who had abandoned a beloved family member, leaving her with three children to rear. I remember Dad refusing the call.

"I don't want to talk to no *nigga* who won't take care of his family," he shouted.

Nigger did not get much play around our house, but that day its usage was justified. According to Dad, the prime characteristic defining a man was the depth of his devotion to family. Anyone who did not measure up was a *nigger*.

So it is understandable why in the early 1950s Dad accepted custody of my stepbrother, Carl, whose mother willingly gave him up. The boy was headed for trouble. A dropout taught by an uncle to steal by the age of nine, he needed discipline and direction, and my dad, the veteran of two wars, was the person to give it. To shirk the responsibility was to be a *nigger*.

My father was born in Camp Hill, Alabama, in 1918. The family relocated to Avondale in Birmingham when he was two. His mother,

Nellie, was born in 1902, and his father, Edward, was born in 1897. I remember Maw-Pat, as we called her, because two long, thick, shiny black braids hung on her chest, a reminder of her Native American Indian and African ancestry. She was primarily a homemaker, but also worked as a housekeeper for $2 a day. Paw-Pat, as he was called, was a cement mason who died long before I was born.

They called my father "Charlie" until he entered Miss Garner's fifth-grade class at Kingston Elementary School. There, his name changed.

"Charlie is the name for a horse," Miss Garner told my father. "Your name is Charles."

My father told his mother Miss Garner's remarks, and forever he was Charles.

Teachers were powerful authority figures in the African-American culture in those days. They shared power with parents, and their word was like law. If a teacher called home to report a child's bad behavior, there was no disputing it. The child would be disciplined at school—and again at home.

The second oldest of five, Dad attended Birmingham's Industrial High School (later renamed Parker High School). After his father went blind, he dropped out to work and support the family. He later earned a GED, enlisted in the military and enrolled in a photography school. He joined the Navy in 1943 during World War II.

"I stayed two years, three months and twenty-seven days," he recalled.

After being discharged from the Navy, Dad met my mother, Rutha, at the home of a mutual friend in Birmingham. They married ten months later in October 1946. He soon joined the Army and was called into the Korean conflict, but my mother was pregnant and encountering financial hardship. An honorable discharge ensued.

Settling into civilian life, Dad first worked at Avondale Mills, then American Cast Iron & Pipe Company (ACIPCO) in 1951. He also bought a house in an area of Birmingham called Washington Heights.

Long since demolished, the neighborhood was once located near the airport and was populated by veterans, teachers and other working-class black citizens. Mom remembers lots of children, neat lawns, fenced-in backyards, pets, vehicles.

"They all had cars and their own homes," she recalled. "Some wives worked and some didn't."

Mom worked as a part-time seamstress at Pizitz department store. My parents owned a two-door Ford. The car was a godsend, literally, as it was the answer to a desperate prayer.

Dad used to trudge through a cemetery in the dark before dawn to catch a bus to ACIPCO. He recalled walking past a black man with "red protruding eyes" on several occasions. He said he prayed for a car, and soon purchased the Ford from his barber for $105.

"Later, murders started happening in the cemetery," he said.

My parents lived in a two-bedroom, one bathroom house at 3221 62nd Street North. But if Dad had had his way, they never would have lived there. He wanted to become a postman in Los Angeles where three friends were waiting.

"I knew I could be a postman in California," he said. "We had friends who were colored postmen and they were making good money."

My mother said he intended to go after they married, but she refused. A Southern girl, attached to her parents, she would say, "Don't go now. We've got to do this, or we've got to do that."

Mom was and remains an attractive lady. Old photographs reveal a woman with wavy shoulder-length hair, smooth brown skin and a sculpted body. They called her "Miss Coca-Cola Bottle" in high school, she said, because her figure resembled the bottle; her round bust and hips accentuated a curiously tiny waistline. After eighty-three years and eight pregnancies, she still has it.

Graduating from Parker High School at the age of sixteen, Mom immediately enrolled in Alabama's Tuskegee Institute and majored in tailoring. She dropped out a year before graduating to marry.

Dad started working in the foundry at ACIPCO as a laborer making large fittings until he injured his leg. Then he became a cook.

By 1954, Birmingham had acquired a dual identity. It was also called Bombingham because of the unusually large number of unsolved, Klan-incited bombings of homes occupied by black families, many of whom had moved into or near areas zoned for whites only.[1]

My father does not remember a lot about the residential bombings. He does confirm racism grew worse in Birmingham after World War II.

"Whites considered blacks uppity, smart, and [they would] say, 'You have to watch this Negro. He just got out of the service.'"

And so, members of the black community watched themselves. "You had to honor those folk. You had to pay them their respect . . . or lose your life," he said.

But that did not hinder black residents from being exemplary citizens and parents. Theirs was a vibrant community that valued education, civic duty, discipline and church.

My parents attended Harmony Street Baptist Church founded in 1888 by twenty-four black men and women from Avondale.[2] The pastor, Reverend M. W. Whitt, would play a major role in rallying community support for my father.

Church was mandatory for black youth back then. Reverence for Jesus Christ as the Savior was instilled at a young age and persisted into adulthood.

"We didn't send our children to church," my father explained. "We took them to church."

Since discipline was so valued, the decision to involve my stepbrother, Carl, in the Boy Scouts just seemed right.

"Everybody was putting their sons in the Boy Scouts," Dad said. "So I wanted to buy him a suit and try to enroll him."

That decision nearly cost my father his life.

2

The Beating Goes On

Early in the afternoon of Saturday, December 11, 1954, my thirty-six-year-old father took Carl, twelve, to Loveman, Joseph and Loeb department store in downtown Birmingham.

The weather was fair. "Nice," Dad recalled.

The store was easy to locate on 19th Street. Finding a place to park was not.

"I couldn't park near the store," he explained. "I drove forever."

Dad finally spotted a man about to leave a space on 18th Street. The man drove off and Dad slipped the car into reverse. Then he noticed something.

"She took the space," he murmured, staring off. Sitting before me, it was as though he had vanished back in time.

A woman had quickly driven into the spot. Dad said he got out of his car and told the woman:

"Ma'am, I was waiting. The man was pulling out and I was backing in." He said the woman yelled back, "I'm getting this spot. My husband is a police officer."

She was Margaret Lynch, wife of Arthur S. Lynch, a patrolman with the Birmingham Police Department. My father said he had remembered seeing her car pass his on the viaduct.

"A raggedy car. Wasn't worth a plug nickel," he added.

A photograph of Mrs. Lynch from the January 27, 1955, edition of the *Birmingham News* showed a smiling woman with dark hair who appeared to be no more than thirty years old.

A deep respect for justice pressed my father that day. Dad said he told Mrs. Lynch that her officer husband was employed to uphold the law.

"He doesn't own the streets of Birmingham," he recalled telling her.

With that, he said he got back into his car and drove off, letting her have the parking space. He eventually found another around the corner.

My father found the Scout suit for Carl at Loveman, Joseph and Loeb, but because Carl did not bring his Scout card, a store clerk would not allow the purchase. Dad left empty-handed, with his pride wounded and a deep sense that trouble was imminent.

My stepbrother never became a Boy Scout. And Dad might have wished he had never tried to make him one.

When he arrived home with Carl, who, according to Dad, was afraid but had said little, he tried to prepare my mother for the worst. He told her what had happened downtown.

"Well, the police may be here after a while," Mom remembered him saying.

My brother, Charles Patrick Jr., who was five at the time of the incident, remembers a loud knock at the door and my father asking who it was. "This is the police. We're looking for Charles Patrick. We have a warrant for your arrest," my brother recalls them saying. He added that my father told my mother "not to worry . . . there must be a mistake."

According to the December 18, 1954, edition of the *Birmingham News*, officers L. L. Marlow and J. P. Renshaw arrested my father that evening at his home on charges of vagrancy and disorderly conduct. He was booked in the city jail at 7:21 p.m. and placed in cell No. 4902.

My mother was relieved that Marlow and Renshaw were the arresting officers. She said they were the neighborhood beat cops who knew the residents and had explained to my father they had to arrest him because there was a warrant. "They didn't do nothin' but just pick him up and take him on down to the station," Mom said.

My father said he saw "the Lord's hand" in that officers other than Lynch came to arrest him. He believed that if Officer Lynch had come to the house, he would have "never made it to jail." Nonetheless, he said he did not trust even the beat officers and was tense and fearful during the ride to jail.

"I thought I was a dead man," my father said. "Because back in those days, the police would pick up black men and lynch them even before they got to jail."

Residents were not the only ones afraid. A police officer in fear of his life once wrote an anonymous letter to his superiors claiming, "The Birmingham police are working the Negro sections as hard as the policy man [insurance salesman] for protection money." The reason for concealing his identity? "I don't want Mr. [Bull] Connor's thugs to shoot me."[1]

African-Americans knew a ride in a Birmingham patrol car might be one's last. And my father said black women were "mistreated" in exchange for lighter sentences. A 1951 incident highlights this fear.

As fifty-one-year-old Bessie Baxter Ammons walked to work, a uniformed officer pulled up next to her and demanded that she get into the patrol car. "No, I ain't going to get in that car," she reportedly responded. Ammons was an employee at the Smithfield Court office. The officer wisely backed off. Historian Glenn T. Eskew wrote: "Bessie Ammons knew better than to get in the car, where in all likelihood she would be beaten, sexually molested, raped or, worst of all, taken to the city jail. For good reason, Birmingham's black people feared the city jail. Prisoners were beaten and sometimes died behind bars."[2]

In another incident, officers J. C. Wilson and J. L. Ray were accused of beating Carl S. Allen in a patrol car en route to jail. When his sister arrived, she found his face "swollen and blue and suffering from other injuries."[3]

Another incident in Eskew's book *But for Birmingham* discusses how the wife of Birmingham Mayor Cooper Green personally witnessed officers "manhandle a prisoner" in 1951. That incident made the press. Most did not.[4]

According to other news accounts, Officer Arthur S. Lynch, thirty-four, and his partner, Officer Jack W. Siniard, thirty-five, were assigned to patrol Birmingham's Southside during the 3–11 p.m. shift on the night of December 11, 1954. But the officers left their beat without authorization and went to the Southside city jail after learning of my father's arrest.[5]

Dad was smoking a cigarette in his cell when suddenly Deputy Warden Earl Jackson, thirty-one, a tall, lanky man, opened it and ordered him out. He told him Lynch wanted to talk to him.

"I wanted to go home. I hadn't done anything to anybody. I was afraid," my father told me.

Once in the hallway, Jackson locked the cell and hall doors. Lynch and Siniard were waiting.

Lynch reportedly asked my father if he had told his wife, Margaret, he didn't care if her husband was a policeman. In that our interviews occurred fifty years after the event, my father did not remember exact verbal exchanges with Lynch that night. Fortunately, the January 27, 1955, edition of the *Birmingham Post-Herald* published his testimony given under oath. "Then Siniard and Jackson grabbed my arms and Lynch told me, 'I'm going to teach you a lesson' . . . Then he started beating on me . . . he was kicking me . . . someone hit me in the back of the neck and I fell . . . someone hit me in the face and kicked me on the head. Then I gave the Masonic distress signal and somebody said, 'Don't hit that boy anymore, you've almost killed him now.' . . . Then they put me back in the cell and Lynch told me, 'I'll see you after the trial on Friday.'"

Eyewitness accounts to the beating painted a more brutal scene.

"I saw Lynch hit him right in the stomach," bricklayer Jim Wilmon told the court, adding that my father got down on his knees with Siniard holding one arm.

"And after Lynch hit him, Patrick fell face first on the floor," Wilmon continued. He also testified that he saw Lynch stomp my father's neck and shoulders and kick him in the side.

Jesse Smiley, a cell mate, was just as graphic in his testimony. He said there was "hollering in the hall and all of us broke for the door.

"The sight we saw was two policemen holding his [Patrick's] arms and a big policeman boxing him with his fists."

Smiley testified that one of the officers twisted my father's left arm behind his back after he fell to the ground.

"The big policeman put his right foot on [Patrick's] neck and kicked him in the head three or four times," Smiley said, adding that my father was bleeding from his mouth, chin and nose after he returned to the cell. "He might have been bleeding inside, too, because his trousers were bloody."[6]

Understandably, my father's memory was fuzzy. He remembered being beaten in a room normally used for prisoner interrogations. But newspaper reports said eyewitnesses saw the beating take place in a second floor hallway of the jail, down the hall from a fingerprint room occupied by half a dozen people at the time.

Also in newspaper accounts, Jackson said he stopped the beating after he saw my father give the Masonic distress signal. Dad remembered Siniard stopping it, but at other times he agreed Jackson did.

I begged Dad to show me the Masonic distress signal. He refused, saying he was no longer a Mason. Subsequent research revealed the distress signal involves "raising both hands and arms to the elbows" while saying, "O Lord, my God! Is there no help for the widow's son?"[7]

I asked if he had uttered those words. "That's what I said," he replied.

I also asked him to discuss what happened after the beating. He said officials offered no medical assistance, nor did his cell mates help.

"The other cell mates would have nothing to do with me. No one did anything [for] me because they were afraid," Dad said.

He remembered two detectives asking about his injuries that night.

"What happened to you, boy?" one inquired. My father said he told them what the officers had done, but realized he had made a mistake when one detective retorted, "What did you say? . . . Did you say 'fall?'"

My father said it appeared he might be in for another beating, so he replied, "Yes, sir, I may have fell."

Newspaper accounts attributed names: Detectives W. M. Prier and J. A. Hale. In statements to Captain J. W. Garrison, both said they saw my father sponging a fresh cut on his chin about 9 p.m., and that he told them "he had fallen off a bunk or fell into something and caused the cut."[8]

Those detectives would get a surprise the following Friday, December 17, 1954.

3
The Accused Is the Accuser

He had a handkerchief. Beset by a steady stream of blood that poured from his chin, that hankie was to become my father's only form of assistance for the next two days.

"I went to town to get my son a Scout suit."

As he lay there bleeding, he might have questioned if he had made the right decision to enroll Carl in the Boy Scouts.

Dad had said he believed the organization would help make a man out of Carl, because a child dropout taught to steal by relatives needed redirecting. But look where his efforts had gotten him.

"I thought my days on earth were done," he said of his ordeal in the Birmingham jail. He did not eat. His mouth was sore, he said.

James Tarlton, incarcerated for bootlegging, penned a song about the place in 1923. In one verse, he wrote, "In twenty-one years, dear, they'll open the door. I'll walk out this jailhouse to do wrong no more."[1]

The song my father sang was in the form of a prayer: "I was praying for the Lord to take care of my wife and my children if I didn't live."

One thing he had—if nothing else—was time to consider the surname of the rude woman with whom he had argued that day. *Lynch.* What irony, the word itself conjuring the fears and fates of countless black Americans. My father once told me, in response to no question I had asked: "You know . . . there was a lot of lynching at that time."

Not the docile type, his parents exhorted him to "stay humble and stay prayerful" in light of the terror imposed by racist whites. Dad recalled familiar incidents from childhood.

"As a boy, we'd walk in the woods and pick up nuts," he said. "And the whites would beat you up so we'd return home another route."

He said on Friday and Saturday nights, the Ku Klux Klan would prowl the neighborhood on horseback, on foot. Robed or hooded, the Taliban of Birmingham mistook themselves for the *posse comitatus*.

"Sometimes they had a thief or someone who stole something and they'd execute them before you. It was scary," my father said. "Mama would make us stay in the house."

Not all blacks did. Dr. Horace Huntley, Director of the Oral History Project at the Birmingham Civil Rights Institute, said as a sixteen-year-old he and friends threw rocks at a KKK procession one night, and then ran home. But every time a car drove by, he felt they were coming after them.

"We would also take the board off the bus and place it farther up so we could sit closer to the front," Huntley said during a January 30, 2004, interview at the Civil Rights Institute. "Sometimes the bus driver would say something, sometimes he wouldn't." One time, a friend threw the sign off the bus.

Mom was eight months pregnant when my father was beaten. She knew nothing about bailing someone out of jail, but from talking to neighbors, she learned.

"I found out that I couldn't get him out for three days," she explained. "They had a law that they could hold him for three days without any charges."

At some point early on, she called my uncle John Lewis—my father's older brother. My uncle contacted Robert E. Bolden, who my father said managed ACIPCO's Pipe Moulders Negro baseball team. Through

Bolden, John Lewis met Malcolm L. Wheeler, a white attorney, who represented many ACIPCO employees. Wheeler, now deceased, secured my father's release from jail within forty-eight hours.

Dad did not remember details of his first meeting with Wheeler, nor did he care that Wheeler was white. He said he felt like he was a "God-sent" man. "And he was," he added.

On a 2007 trip to Birmingham, I toured the offices of the firm where Malcolm Wheeler once practiced to learn more about the man who took my father's case.

There on the wall was a succession of Wheeler luminaries—three generations—all hailing from the legal profession. I could see the dominant family traits—eyes located close to the bridges of their noses, handsome men. Wheeler's father, Robert J. Wheeler, a circuit court judge, was once described as a "stern man who went straight to the day's docket with little wasted motion."[2] But it was my father's advocate whose image captivated me.

Debonair and refined, Malcolm Wheeler was dressed like Humphrey Bogart in *Casablanca,* sporting a trench coat and fedora. His eyes, which conveyed determination, were gripping.

Wheeler was a devout Methodist, a founding member of Wilson Chapel Methodist Church in Roebuck and a philanthropist.[3]

My father said his brother took him straight home after Wheeler bailed him out on Monday, December 13.

"I was scared to go anywhere else," he said.

He remembered fear when he entered the house. With blood on his shirt, face swollen, he said my sister, Rutha Jr., seven at the time, grabbed him and asked, "Daddy, are you all right?"

"I said, 'Daddy is all right.'"

"His chin was puffed up," my mother recalled. "And his face . . . one side of his face was swollen up." She said she did not find out until the moment he came home that he had been beaten. "I didn't know he had had that kind of treatment down there."

Efforts to discover what others in the family recalled about the incident were disappointing.

My stepbrother, Carl, died in 1995, prior to the start of interviews for this book. Unfortunately, my father could only recall Carl's fear, no opinions he had expressed.

Charles Jr., five at the time, remembered nothing about Dad's return home from jail. His recollections centered on the time of the initial arrest. Likewise, Larry, who was four, recalled nothing, except playing cowboy games. He remembered no trouble.

My stepsister, Christine, who at the time was nine and who did not live with my father, could only recall the talk around town, which was "that there was one parking spot, and Dad and a white lady were going for it and Daddy beat her to it. Then all hell broke loose."

Ironically, Gregory, who at two was the youngest, recalled emotions, movement. He said my mother was crying a lot, and he was left in a crib, other kids running amuck in the living room. He also remembered visiting different homes.

The day after my father was bailed out of jail, John Lewis took him to ACIPCO's staff physician where he received six stitches in his chin. Company records showed that Dr. Crayton C. Fargason Jr. was the attending physician. However, a statement my father gave to Captain J. W. Garrison of the Birmingham Police Department specified that Dr. C. J. Fisher was the ACIPCO doctor who examined him. It is unclear whether Dad misspoke concerning the doctor's surname, but one fact appears certain: Newspaper reports said he remained under the doctor's care for months and was only able to work a total of nine days between December 13, 1954, and January 29, 1955.[4]

Though he suffered no broken bones, Dad said he was sore all over, having been kicked and stomped in his private parts, back and legs. In addition, he endured severe headaches and bouts of spitting up blood. As well as the physical pain, there was the mental agony leading up to

Friday, December 17, the date of his court appearance. The most daunting question of the day was: Would he tell?

"The blacks back then were afraid to say that they were beaten," Dad explained. But what did his associates, including his attorney, advise?

"Malcolm Wheeler told me to 'Tell the truth,' and Robert Bolden said, 'Tell the truth [even] if you die.'"

My father clearly recalled the advice of Jessie Taggart, an ACIPCO employee and brother of prominent black dentist Dr. Ernest W. Taggart.

"If you die, tell the truth about what these people did to you," my father remembered Taggart saying. "If it's God's will that you live, you will live to tell your children about what happened to you."

It was understood my mother would not accompany Dad to court. And he did not discuss the incident much with her. In fact, she said in the 1950s, black men generally did not discuss grave topics with their wives, much less involve them in tense courtroom situations—especially when they were pregnant.

"That's about the way black men were with women. Now they would talk to other men, but they didn't say much to women," Mom said. "I don't know if it was like that in all marriages, but it seemed like that was the way it was in most marriages."

Yet the agony of this moral should-I-tell-it-all dilemma and the final answer to it had to come from a soul mate.

That Thursday night Dad went to bed, but not to sleep.

"What should I do tomorrow when I go to court?" my mother vaguely recalled him asking—in the middle of the night. She said she did not remember the answer she gave, but he later told her she had responded, "Tell the truth."

"I was half sleep, but that sounds like something I would have said if I had been consciously awake." She laughed.

For all the complexity of the era, they were simple people who believed and practiced simple principles. Read your Bible. Believe in Jesus.

Obey your parents. Obey the law. Fulfill your civic duty. Submit to your husband. Love your wife, your children. Tell the truth.

"I believe that truth [is] the winning power over anything," my mother explained. "I really believe that, still believe that, always believe that. Truth was all I ever knew. Tell the truth."

So early Friday morning, December 17, Charles Patrick eased out of bed without awakening Rutha and headed for the courthouse in his Ford sedan. There he joined Malcolm Wheeler, and the two stood before Judge Ralph E. Parker. Their destinies entwined.

My father had said Judge Parker was "a hater of Negroes," a segregationist.

In a 1957 case, Judge Parker ruled against attorney Arthur Shores and civil rights activist Fred Shuttlesworth in their attempt to defy Birmingham's segregation bus ordinance. In a March 21, 1957, opinion, Judge Parker wrote: "Segregation had been established by God, and was essential to harmonious race relations as northern cities with large black populations would very soon discover . . . I cannot conceive how any right-thinking person who understands the conditions that exist in the South can advocate abandoning our segregation laws, when such a course will inevitably lead to racial amalgamation and mongrelization."[5]

Parker was also called "Birmingham's judicial Will Rogers" because of his courtroom wit. Parker once commented to a courtroom audience that "90 percent of my cases here have to do with liquor." So when Parker learned that one defendant scheduled to appear in court on a drinking charge had been hit and killed by a train, he quipped, "Let's hope he wasn't drunk when he died."[6]

But Parker also had a reputation for issuing fair verdicts. In so doing, he garnered the hatred of former Police Commissioner Eugene "Bull" Connor. Connor is remembered for his 1963 barbaric police-dog tactics against civil rights protestors, antics that cast national light on the movement.

Judge Parker won a 1952 legal joust with Connor, a defeat that influenced Connor's decision not to run for police commissioner in 1953. Parker found Connor guilty of "disorderly conduct, joint occupancy of a room with a member of the opposite sex, and extramarital sexual intercourse," and sentenced him to 180 days in jail plus a $100 fine— overturned later by the Alabama Supreme Court.[7]

Connor accused Parker of plotting revenge because earlier Connor had not only opposed his appointment to the bench, but had led a campaign for his removal from it.[8]

By 1954, this vitriolic melee led to a more progressive police commissioner at the helm, one dedicated to cleaning up the cesspool of corruption Connor had created and allowed to fester in the police department. Commissioner Robert E. Lindbergh was in power by the time my father and Wheeler stood before Judge Parker that day.

Blacks who appeared before judges swollen, bruised and battered generally gave the same answer when asked about visible injuries.

"I fell, Your Honor" was the standard reply.

Dad knew it well and out of fear had muttered the same to Detectives Prier and Hale following his pounding in the jail. From conversations with him throughout my life, two factors surfaced about that day.

First, he believed that because he had served the United States in two wars, the country owed him the same respect given to white veterans. Second, he passionately wanted justice for himself and any other person brutalized by police officers in uniform.

I asked my father to recall as best he could his thoughts as he stood before the judge.

"I said, 'Well, if I die, I'm going to be with my Father, so I told the truth,'" he explained. "They said if you lose your life, go ahead and tell the truth and be a man."

In addition to my father, all involved parties were present that day: detectives Prier and Hale, Mrs. Lynch, arresting officers Marlow and Renshaw, Malcolm Wheeler and officers Siniard and Lynch, who, according to court records, was called as a witness by the defendant.[9]

Birmingham Post-Herald police reporter Bill Mobley who was also on hand offered his own courtroom observation: "The complainant had a cut on his chin which he said was a result of the beating."[10]

The trial began with my father pleading innocent to charges of disorderly conduct, the vagrancy charge having been dropped the Monday before the trial. That was followed by Detective Prier's testimony, after which Mrs. Lynch took the stand.

She told the court that Patrick backed up, blocking her attempt to park, stuck his head out of the window and yelled that he wanted the parking space for which she had been waiting. Mrs. Lynch said he exited his car, walked to her car window, began cursing at her, walked to the rear of her car, saw a police tag back there, returned to her window, cursed her some more, hopped back into his car, drove forward then roared into reverse, crashed into the front grill of her car, hopped back out of the car, pressed his face to her car window, cursed more, threatened her, rattled the handle of her car—and then drove off.

Her testimony was a twisted tale of conflicting statements that Wheeler patiently and laboriously unraveled, humor notwithstanding.

"There were lots of people in town out shopping, weren't they?" Wheeler asked.

"I don't know anything about the people in downtown," she quipped.

"You say this defendant's car was in front of you, wasn't it?" Wheeler continued.

"No, he wasn't in front of me, he was sitting at the red light."

"Well, that's, well he was in front of you or in back of you?" he asked.

"Well, he had to be in front of me," she said.

"Alright then, he was in front of you. His car was in front of your car?" Wheeler asked.

"Not in front of mine, no sir."

"Well, let me start again. Now, Mrs. Lynch, we want to clarify it now, was his car in the front of your car? Or in the back of your car?"

Wheeler also questioned Officer Marlow and Detective Prier before calling my father to the stand.

Dad told a different story from Mrs. Lynch's, one that had him communicating with the driver who had initially exited the space, leaving it for him. He testified that Mrs. Lynch blocked his attempt to back into the space when she pulled her car forward. He confirmed that he did exit his car, but only once—to tell her that he had been waiting for the space and that he did not care if her husband was a policeman in reply to her taunt. He insisted he never rammed his vehicle into Mrs. Lynch's, never cursed her. He said he only drove off, finding a space around the corner in front of the Federal Reserve building, leaving the parking space for her.

Dad also mentioned his disappointment in not being able to purchase the Boy Scout suit because Carl had not brought his Scout identification card. He then related details of the arrest later that night by officers Marlow and Renshaw, and the subsequent violent encounter at the city jail.

While my father did not identify Officer Siniard in court that day, he did point out Officer Lynch as the one who pummeled him in the hall outside cell 4902. He spoke of his bruises, the fact that he vomited blood afterward and the note from ACIPCO's Dr. Fisher that he kept in his pocket. He also mentioned the Masonic distress signal that stopped the beating, but he said he did not know who exactly stopped it.[11]

Parker and Prier both questioned my father on the matter of whether he had fallen off a bunk in the cell, causing the cut to his chin, or whether he "had been whipped" by someone. My father was not forthcoming, saying he did not recall what he had told them.

Wheeler later questioned Lynch and Siniard. Lynch said he could not remember being at the jail the night of December 11. Siniard was more forthright, insisting that he and Lynch absolutely did not venture to the jail at all that night.[12]

The officers might have been able to pull it off had it not been for the Birmingham Police Department's notorious corruption in general and the reputations of Lynch and Siniard in particular.

Both the *Birmingham News* and *Birmingham World* documented an earlier incident involving a woman named Frankie Merritt. Lynch and Siniard were said to have searched her home for illegal whiskey. Siniard reportedly slapped her; Lynch allegedly broke her sofa in the search. In court, the officers produced a bottle of whiskey they said was taken from her tub. Merritt maintained the tub was filled with water.[13]

Judge Parker had previously fined Merritt $25 for violating the city's liquor laws, but in light of new revelations about the two arresting officers, defense attorney Harold P. Knight, a white man, filed a motion for Parker to dismiss his judgment against Merritt. Knight argued that "in view of the Patrick case, [the officers] were immediately thereafter proved unreliable under oath." Unfortunately, Merritt settled for the $25 fine because she feared "bodily harm" if she pressed charges against Siniard and Lynch.[14]

To his credit, Judge Parker agreed to take my father's case under advisement until December 30, though he did permit the charges to stand, attaching a $25 fine.

Wheeler immediately filed a formal complaint with Birmingham Police Chief G. L. Pattie, who instructed Captain Garrison to "get to the bottom of it."[15]

Garrison wasted no time. Transcripts from court records detailed several statements my father, Deputy Warden E. J. Jackson, Lynch and Siniard gave to Garrison concerning the beating. The interrogations began on December 17 after the trial.

My father gave his statement to Garrison at 3:30 p.m. in Room 116 of city hall. It was similar to statements he made in court, except that he added that he bled all night after the beating.

Next was Jackson at 10:10 p.m. Present were Sergeant C. D. Guy and Warden C. T. Lamar in addition to Garrison. Jackson confirmed that he escorted Lynch and Siniard to Patrick's cell. He also said he stopped the beating but did not remember whether my father was bleeding, nor did he think he needed medical attention because he saw no injuries.

Siniard and Lynch appeared together at 10:30 p.m. before both Garrison and Guy, but Lynch refused to give a statement. Siniard stressed that he "had never seen the Negro before today in court."[16]

The following day, December 18, Lynch returned to city hall with his attorney, J. G. Adams, and gave a statement to Assistant Police Chief Jamie Moore at 4:15 p.m. During Moore's interrogation, Lynch finally admitted going to the jail with Siniard. He also confirmed that he hit Patrick "three or four times" on the "left side of his head and his left arm" and that Patrick fell in a corner.[17]

With Lynch's statement, Pattie could boast that within twenty-four hours of issuing the directive, his subordinates had indeed gotten to the bottom of it.

4

Press Attack on
the Devil's Department

Despite the implications of the surname Lynch, it inspired no terror in
Charles Patrick. Everything about him—family, religious and community values, coupled with military training—came into play, beckoning
truth be told, consequences be damned.

My mother said she was afraid when she awoke after my father had
left for court because she did not remember what she had told him in the
middle of the night. Indeed, she never realized the full impact of what
she had advised until December 18, 1954, when "Man Testifies in Court
Officer Beat Him," and "Chief Orders Investigation into Charge That
Officer Beat Prisoner," blared on the front pages of the *Birmingham News*
and *Birmingham Post-Herald* respectively.

Dad could not have taken his stand at a better time in the city's
history.

The Birmingham City Commission was more moderate in its makeup
than in the past. Police Commissioner Robert E. Lindbergh had re-
placed racist Eugene "Bull" Connor, and Public Improvement Commissioner Wade Bradley was in for segregationist Jabo Waggoner. In addition, independent-thinking business owners had organized a decade
earlier into an effective group known as the Young Men's Business Club.
A group of white merchants, lawyers, publishers, engineers, architects
and the like, they advocated civic reform and racial diversification of

Birmingham's economic base. Finally, powerful players in white-owned newsrooms were not afraid to take positions opposing the city polity.

The *Birmingham News* and the *Birmingham Post-Herald* functioned under a joint-operating agreement in 1954. The *Post-Herald,* the morning paper, was owned by Scripps Howard; the *News,* the evening paper, was owned by S. I. Newhouse. According to J. Mills Thornton III in his book, *Dividing Lines,* James E. Mills—*Post-Herald* editor and president—was a "close associate of the business progressives" and the *News* publisher, Clarence Hanson, "was one of their leaders."[1]

The view that Hanson was a progressive was not shared by all. Howell Raines, who authored *My Soul Is Rested,* said the *Birmingham News* under Hanson was not "noted for being racially progressive."[2]

Joe Dickson, a real estate consultant who in 1990 acquired the rights to the black community's *Birmingham World,* was even more forthright. "From 1953–1955, the position of that newspaper *[Birmingham News]* didn't do anything good for black folk. To me, it was a combination of advertising and whatever the power structure wanted them to do."[3]

Nonetheless, the *Birmingham News* took unprecedented stands throughout my father's trial, stands that included front-page coverage coupled with bold editorial positions.

It should be noted that a significant link existed between the black-owned *Birmingham World* and the Birmingham chapter of the National Association for the Advancement of Colored People (NAACP). Emory O. Jackson, managing editor of the *World* at that time, also served as one of NAACP's executive committee members. Jackson's role would become more important as my father's trial heated up in January 1955 and mass meetings were organized on his behalf at Sixteenth Street Baptist Church.[4]

Birmingham's press had become accustomed to taking opposing positions against the city's police department ever since Detective Henry Darnell caught former police commissioner "Bull" Connor in a sexual tryst with Christina Brown in December 1951. Afterward, the *Birming-*

ham News demanded his resignation, arguing, "Mr. Connor cannot do the kind of job that is needed in his high office. Conditions within his department cannot be what they should be so long as he continues in office."[5]

The *Post-Herald* wrote, "If complete reorganization of the police department, after necessary firings or resignations, is required to restore public confidence and lift the morale of the honest, hard-working officers remaining, then the sooner that job is done the better."[6]

Connor had no qualms about involving others in plots to destroy his enemies, such as Judge Parker, who presided over my father's trial.

The February 19, 1952, "Report of Citizen's Committee on Birmingham Police Department" confirmed Connor's bold and unethical campaign to oust Parker. Several police detectives and officers accused Connor of treating them unfairly in retaliation for their refusal "to sign a petition for the discharge of Judge Parker of the Recorder's Court."[7]

That the Ku Klux Klan had infiltrated the department was undeniable; Connor maintained a close relationship with them. One historian wrote, "Without question he knew Klansmen, associated with them, sought and accepted their support, and habitually let them have their way with people of color in Birmingham."[8]

And as if Connor's indiscretions were not enough, the department continued giving police reporters like the *Post-Herald*'s Bill Mobley and others much to write about.

The Birmingham Police Department was but a reflection of the officers who comprised it. I was not looking for articles to support that notion, but during the years spent pouring through books, microfiche and Birmingham City Commission archives, I encountered dozens of articles about officers arrested for this, on trial for that.

On December 7, 1954, former police officer Robert G. Luttrell stood trial on charges of burglary and grand larceny. He was acquitted a day later. Two months later, Chief Pattie charged Officer J. L. McCain with "conduct unbecoming a police officer" in association with a stolen gasoline tanker. Pattie relieved McCain from duty. The tanker was later found with more than two thousand gallons of gasoline missing. McCain's wife operated a gas station.[9]

Also in February 1955, Officer J. E. Smith lost "several off-days owed him as the result of 'tactless and unfortunate choice of words'" during the arrest of a nineteen-year-old woman. Sergeant James W. Morris and Officer Bobby W. Montgomery were both fired in the fall of 1954 for theft. In March 1955, the Jefferson County Civil Service Personnel Board upheld the firing of former officer Batson W. Noble, who was dismissed for "drinking a beer in a burglarized establishment." That same month, Lieutenant E. E. Loveless was temporarily removed from the force for fighting with restaurateur B. L. Bright inside his Huntsville establishment. Loveless was later demoted to police sergeant.[10]

Glenn T. Eskew noted in *But for Birmingham* other serious incidents involving police officers. A sergeant and six officers were caught in the act of prying open a safe at the Blue Diamond Company. They were cleared of wrongdoing in October 1953. That same month, Officer Paul Beddow was fired in connection with an armed robbery of a gas station. A month later, two officers were charged with grand larceny in connection with a break-in at a furniture company. According to Eskew, "...neither officer had served more than two years." A year later, a police officer burglary ring was quashed, revealing twenty-three policemen linked to forty-one crimes netting $50,000. It was "estimated that 45 percent of the force received payoffs, 45 percent would have accepted them if offered, and only 10 percent steadfastly refused to be bought off."[11]

When Connor was once told that some of the burglaries might be inside jobs, he quipped, "Only legitimate holdups will be investigated," giving criminally inclined officers carte blanche to so engage.[12]

Jackson's attesting to his participation in the assault coupled with Lynch's confession to beating Patrick effectively painted Siniard (who had denied being at the jail altogether) a liar. With ammunition to act,

Pattie did just that, promptly firing Lynch and Siniard for conduct un-becoming officers and suspending Jackson for ten days. Though Jackson opened my father's cell and held one of his arms, somehow Pattie deemed a ten-day suspension adequate because he was credited with stopping the attack. Nevertheless, his "failure to immediately report the incident" coupled with his "failure to see that the prisoner received medical atten-tion" earned Jackson the suspension. In response to the beating, Pattie also instituted a new policy at the city jail requiring policemen visiting inmates to sign a permanent roster.[13]

City politicians were clearly paranoid over what the Northern press might make of the Patrick case. Mayor James W. Morgan once quipped, "All of this will be seized hungrily by the Northern press and some trouble-making groups."[14]

His fears were not completely unfounded. My father said the story re-ceived nationwide coverage.

In July 2007, I interviewed former *Post-Herald* reporter Andrew Glaze, who at eighty-seven was finishing a novel. He said the two news-papers relied on competing syndicates for news. The *Birmingham News* used Associated Press (AP), and the *Post-Herald* used United Press (UP). Correspondents from the AP definitely covered the Patrick case, lending credence to a story my mother told me.

She said a reporter who wrote the story about the FBI's plan to "probe charges officers beat prisoner,"[15] was sent from New York, worked for AP and told my father he was glad he had reported the beating. She also said the reporter had been waiting for an African-American to publicly ac-cuse police of the brutality courtroom watchers knew happened regu-larly. She said the reporter intended for the story to go national. It did, by way of the AP wire.

The *Selma Times-Journal* ran an AP story on the front page of its De-cember 21, 1954, edition that included the FBI connection. Chicago's *Jet* magazine published a piece about the Patrick incident in its De-cember 30, 1954, edition. The *Atlanta Daily World* ran a front-page story in its December 31, 1954, edition; and the *Chicago Defender* ran stories about the incident through October 1955.

Special Agent James A. Robey of the FBI was quoted in the December 21, 1954, edition of the *Birmingham News* saying that an investigation had been launched to "show if the jail attack had deprived the prisoner of any of his constitutional freedoms." Then strangely, more than a week later, Robey hushed. *Post-Herald* police reporter Bill Mobley would write, "Nothing has been heard from the FBI here, since Agent-in-Charge James A. Robey announced over a week ago that the case was being investigated."[16] The case was eventually tried in federal court, albeit months later.

Robey's son, James A. Robey Jr., said his father was in charge of the FBI's Birmingham office from 1953 to 1955, and died in 1972. Robey Jr., who still lives in Alabama, said his father was a Christian who "saw people [African-Americans] as part of a group, but he was very dedicated to a sense of right and wrong, and that overrode that sense of [a person] being black."[17]

At first it appeared my father would quickly prevail over the officers, but the politicians had other ideas.

In 1954, Birmingham city politics consisted of a three-man oligarchy: one mayor and two commissioners. Mayor James Morgan—who was also commission president—Public Improvement Commissioner Wade Bradley and Public Safety Commissioner Robert Lindbergh comprised the Birmingham City Commission. Typical of an assembly, some of its members voted as a unit. So it was with Morgan and Bradley.

In that Lindbergh was committed to cleaning up Birmingham's police department, it was not surprising that he supported Pattie's decision to fire Lynch and Siniard. But when Lindbergh sought support from Morgan and Bradley to turn the matter over to the civil service personnel board, they refused, prompting Lindbergh to introduce a resolution on December 27, 1954, recommending that Siniard and Lynch be fired.[18]

Perhaps Lindbergh knew intuitively the other commissioners would not support his attempt to permanently end the officers' careers, thus the move to let the personnel board have the final say. For Morgan and Bradley it was about power. Or so they said.

"I think it is our responsibility to take action one way or the other," said Morgan, with Bradley adding he was not in favor "of passing any more of our power on to the board."[19]

When the day came for a vote, December 28, 1954, Morgan and Bradley voted to reinstate the officers with only a thirty-day suspension, citing the "good records of both Lynch and Siniard." That was followed by Jefferson County Civil Service Director Ray Mullins's declaration that he would "not press charges against two Birmingham policemen who beat a Negro prisoner at City Jail on December 11." The city commission's actions were also recorded in the personnel board's meeting minutes of December 29, 1954.[20]

Lindbergh felt betrayed and questioned whether they had not just given "each of our four hundred officers permission to go to the jail and beat one prisoner each."[21]

It should not have been surprising that Bradley voted the way he did. A news brief in the January 5, 1955, edition of the *Birmingham Post-Herald* offered an explanation for the way things turned out. "Bradley generally sides with Morgan in commission disputes, but on one or two occasions he has voted with Lindbergh against the mayor."[22]

Lindbergh and the departments under his control were clearly on the wrong end of a double standard. In his challenge to Morgan and Bradley, he questioned why they possessed sole power to discipline employees in their respective areas, but the same did not hold true for police and firefighters.

"I want my department to be treated the same as others," Lindbergh said. This public challenge prompted Morgan to declare that he intended to ask the state legislature to "give each commissioner sole power of discipline within his department" and that he would like for city employees to take their disciplinary appeals directly to the civil service board, not the city commission.[23]

It was a move that did nothing to mend the breach, however. Lindbergh reportedly left the meeting and did not return.[24]

In *But for Birmingham,* Eskew wrote, "By not backing up Lindbergh, the other two commissioners in effect compromised his authority."[25]

The attorneys for Lynch and Siniard were, respectively, James G. Adams and C. E. "Bud" Huey, the latter of whom was a product of the Birmingham Police Department.

As a police captain, Huey had accumulated several traffic violations, one involving a one-hundred-mile-an-hour high speed chase in which Leeds, Alabama, police chased him back to Birmingham on July 26, 1952. An Alabama highway patrolman who joined the pursuit hit another car, killing a woman. Charges from that incident included "speeding, passing on a hill, and failure to yield the right of way to an emergency vehicle." Huey resigned from the police department on July 29, 1952, and opened a law firm a month later. He was convicted of speeding and fined $100 in October of that year.[26]

A public hearing prior to the city commissioner's vote allowed Huey and Adams, along with veterans' organization leader Joe Denaburg, to speak on behalf of Lynch and Siniard. It worked, for after city commissioners voted for the officers' suspension, personnel board director Ray Mullins told a reporter, "I assume this is the end of the matter," even before his board had ever formally received the matter. In addition to each seeking mercy for Lynch and Siniard, Adams added that he had "talked with Patrick and that Patrick 'assured me he didn't want these officers prosecuted.'"[27]

If oaths had been administered at public hearings, Adams would have perjured himself. My father had said he not only wanted to see the officers fired, but also incarcerated because he said they were criminals. He dismissed any thought that his color would be an obstacle to achieving this end and thus any unfavorable ruling was met with greater resolve to challenge it.

And so, unable to work, spitting up blood and suffering cruel headaches, Charles Patrick regrouped with Malcolm Wheeler and readied for another round. Neither of them realized that the least likely of soldiers was donning armor to join them.

5
Citizen Soldiers Aim and Write

Patrick's truth to power was the kindling that set Birmingham's political establishment ablaze. Certainly Mayor Morgan and Commissioner Bradley felt the heat after voting to reinstate officers Lynch and Siniard.

The *Birmingham Post-Herald* was the first to denounce their actions on December 29 and 30, 1954, via an editorial and John Temple Graves's column respectively. The editorial exposed the fallacy of restoring Lynch and Siniard to the police force.

"If justice was served by reinstatement of two police officers who entered the city jail and beat a prisoner held there then we do not understand the meaning of the word." A strong indictment followed. "There is no excuse for the officers' action. There is no excuse for the jail warden who permitted them to enter the prisoner's cell. A policeman's badge and uniform do not give him license to beat and bully a prisoner and one who does it has no place on the police force. Race, color or provocation does not enter into the consideration."[1]

Graves's column, published in the December 30 edition of the *Post-Herald,* set the tone for nearly every citizen letter written in response to Morgan's and Bradley's decision to reinstate Lynch and Siniard. Logic watertight, Graves wrote: "What sort of standard calls it 'tempering justice with mercy' when so-called officers of the law who have been guilty of seeking out a prisoner in jail and beating him up are let off with a mere slap on the wrist in spite of the proper wish of the police chief and the commissioner of police that the men be dropped from the service? This deed disgraced . . . the two men at the time but official condonance now disgraces the city of Birmingham and the Southern states. This case calls for reopening by public outcry."[2]

Graves got his public outcry. Paper flowed in the form of letters to the commissioners, letters to the mayor and letters to the editor—from Birmingham's white citizenry.

Attorney Jerome A. Cooper of Cooper, Mitch & Black penned a December 30 letter to Lindbergh and Pattie commending their stand. "Most people applaud your position in the regrettable case of the Negro prisoner who was beaten in jail. And I believe that they deplore the apparent disposition of Commissioners Morgan and Bradley to treat gross official misconduct very lightly."[3]

Former *New York Times* editor Howell Raines, a Birmingham native, said in a July 17, 2007, telephone interview that Cooper would have been considered a progressive by Birmingham's standards. His firm represented out-of-state labor unions.

"They [Cooper and his firm] exercised a much greater freedom of speech because they couldn't be pressured by the local establishment," Raines said.

One citizen, Mrs. Marlowe Riggins, who acknowledged supporting Mayor Morgan in the past, berated him in her letter for downplaying theft in the city garage, accusing him of leaving "all the dirty work for Lindbergh to do." She then berated him on his light treatment of Lynch and Siniard. "In regard to the two policemen who beat up a Negro named Patrick, it is your attitude that makes for race hatred . . . I have seen many white people who shove colored people around just because they can and men like you and Bradley . . . uphold them. Shame on you for such conduct."[4]

A *Birmingham News* editorial invited citizens to question the fairness and logic of reinstating the officers who admitted to the beating. "Do we want men of this attitude of mind enforcing our laws? Do we want police officers who show such lack of self-control? . . . Should it [the city] keep on the police force officers who fail to control themselves first of all?"[5]

Unitarian church minister Alfred W. Hobart penned in response: "May I add my commendation for the position you have taken in your editorial columns in connection with the recent jail beating incident?"[6]

Citizen Sidney Williams wrote, "I agree with the *Birmingham News* for once." In praising the *News* for its editorial, Mrs. Harold Jacobs wanted the editors to know that she was expressing "the sentiment of many around" her.[7]

One citizen, who chose to remain anonymous, mailed the editorial to Mayor Morgan and wrote across the top, "I am sure that every right thinking person in Birmingham agrees with this editorial."[8]

Indeed, Morgan was lashed with the pen and shrill of citizens who reminded him of how he had achieved power.

"I can say one thing. I voted and worked for you in the last election but I surely will vote against you and work against you twice as diligently in the future. You have given blanket permission for all policemen to beat up anybody they want to without reason and receive a short suspension," wrote citizen D. Q. Harpless.[9]

Mae Young called Morgan's decision to reinstate "the most disgraceful thing," then echoed Harpless's sentiments, "I think the people who vote will remember it when the next election comes along."[10]

Robert H. Loeb, president of the Young Men's Business Club of Birmingham, a group of white reformist businessmen, informed Morgan in his letter of a resolution the club passed deploring "the recent brutal treatment of a prisoner in our City Jail." YMBC called for the city commission to take steps to prevent all brutality against prisoners in custody and commended Lindbergh and Pattie for their brave stand.[11]

My mother believed the city commission's leniency with Lynch and Siniard sent the wrong message to children, and she said that angered parents.

"The children looked up to the officers and because of all the press, they knew they had to punish those officers—for the sake of Birmingham's children," she said. "They were ashamed of the police because they didn't want their children to have a negative view of the police."

Mom echoed a sentiment expressed in Homer L. Thomas's commentary published in the *Birmingham Post-Herald.* Thomas was closely associated with the Character Education Program, taught in Birmingham schools, so he knew firsthand that children had been instructed to respect "constituted authority." Thus the conclusion in his communiqué that if two policemen can get away with beating up a prisoner in jail, "what can we expect of our impulsive youngsters amid the excitement of athletic events, or when they meet perhaps, at some drive-in café after the game?"[12]

Thomas also impugned Morgan's sense of justice, first by assailing the mayor's mishandling of monetary irregularities at the city garage. He then declared that Morgan's and Bradley's thirty-day suspension for Lynch and Siniard "was more like 'tampering' with justice than tempering it." He ended with a bold inquisition. "Have we not the right to demand straightforward, honest and courageous handling of disciplinary cases without a suspicion of politics or favoritism and a little more team work at the city hall?"[13]

In his January 3, 1955, letter to the *Birmingham News,* Rufus A. Points Jr. made reference to a popular WBRC radio program called *The People Speak,* which aired December 28, 1954. He wanted Morgan and Bradley to know that the citizens who called in to express their dissatisfaction over the thirty-day suspension of Lynch and Siniard were some of the same citizens "who were interested enough to go to the polls and vote these commissioners in office." Mrs. J. E. Hall referenced the same radio program in her letter to Morgan: "The opinion was about 4 to 1 that the policemen who left their posts of duty to enter the jail to beat up a prisoner and then falsify about it when first questioned could not be trusted." Then she slammed Mrs. Lynch, who she said, "took advantage of the fact that her husband was a policeman."[14]

Other bold citizens who signed their names on letters sent to Morgan and newspaper editors included Mrs. A. S. Davis, J. C. Long and Henry L. Jones. In one way or another, all assailed Morgan and Bradley for going easy on Lynch and Siniard.

But perhaps one of the most penetrating sentiments expressed by Birmingham's white-owned press was John Temple Graves's column of January 6, 1955. The column followed a *Post-Herald* article the day before whereby Lindbergh and Morgan were reportedly trying to mend their breach after the latter voted to reinstate the officers.[15]

Graves wrote: "If the promised 'unity' among our city commissioners means Commissioner Lindbergh and Police Chief Pattie will be expected to yield to the majority in such flagrant mistakes as substituting a slap on the wrist for the real punishment they proposed in the monstrous Patrick jail-beating case, We-the-People prefer discord."[16]

At its January 16, 1955, meeting at Sixteenth Street Baptist Church, the NAACP adopted a resolution commending Lindbergh and Pattie, but denouncing Morgan and Bradley. A full report of my father's case was presented at the highly publicized meeting, which reportedly "overflowed the main floor of spacious Sixteenth Street Baptist Church." My father remembered attending the meeting, but did not recall speaking. However, newspaper reports said Dad's pastor, Harmony Street Baptist Church Pastor M. W. Whitt, did address the crowd.[17]

Some Birmingham citizens can still remember the hoopla surrounding the beating case. Arthur Walton, my father's friend for over fifty years and former ACIPCO employee, said it was a big deal, the talk of the town, because of the race issue.

"Not a lot of black men would accuse officers," said Walton, an ACIPCO retiree for more than a decade. He added that it was unusual for white citizens to become incensed over police brutality against a black man.[18]

"Just think about it. To challenge that at that time, that was phenomenal," explained *Birmingham World* owner Joe Dickson. "You just didn't do that and that was probably the reason [for the public outcry]." Dickson believed it was the public that drove front-page news coverage of the case, not the newspaper staffers. "The newspapers were blindsided by the public and therefore opposed the establishment."[19]

One historian believed Commissioner Lindbergh was the reason Dad's case remained in the media. J. Mills Thornton III noted, "Never before had Birmingham's institutions been willing to stand so determinedly behind a black man in a dispute with a police officer. It was clear that the principal reason that this incident had not been dismissed, as so many like it had been in the past, was Commissioner Lindbergh." Yet the contributions of Police Chief Pattie cannot be ignored. It was Pattie who ordered Captain Garrison to conduct interrogations that led to confessions, and it was Pattie, along with Lindbergh, who fired Lynch and Siniard.[20]

Of the firing and public shrieking following the officers' reinstatement, Dr. Horace Huntley said it was unusual for that to take place. Huntley, the University of Alabama at Birmingham History professor, added, "We could speak with people in this [my father's] age group who have seen worse things but it did not get picked up by the newspapers."[21]

Huntley believed that whites were outraged because they were isolated from what was happening to African-Americans at that time. They did not realize such beatings were not unusual occurrences, Birmingham being the most segregated big city in the country back then, he said. "Whites had blinders on. They knew the general society, but they didn't know how black folk lived on a daily basis."[22]

Granted some whites genuinely may not have known how blacks lived, yet at least one openly boasted about her fellow white citizens' color-blind responses to the Patrick beating. Mrs. J. E. Hall, in her missive to Mayor Morgan, called herself "a dyed-in-the-wool Southerner," who was proud "of the justice and lack of prejudice of those Southern people on that [*The People Speak* radio] broadcast."[23]

On the other hand, it would be erroneous to assume the majority of white citizens in Birmingham supported Patrick. Though ACIPCO was founded "as an experiment in Christian industrial democracy" to promote "biracial communication," Walton remembered there was bitterness toward my father, whose supervisor was white. Though Dad never admitted this to me, Walton remembered that my father "and his supervisor got into it . . . Not all the white people were for him. If they were, they wouldn't say anything about it either way."[24]

Huntley echoed the fact that many citizens might have tacitly approved the officers' actions. "The vast majority of people who wrote letters against what the officers did were in the minority," he said.[25]

One man actually wrote a letter in support of the Birmingham jail. In 1955, a traveling salesman wanted to let the public know about the "nice treatment" he received while in the Birmingham jail. The man, who signed his name "Salesman," said he had overheard several other people, "both white and colored," discussing how "everyone over there was very nice and they were doing all they could to make them comfortable during their stay there." "Salesman" went on to say that he had not heard anyone complain about ill treatment during his incarceration. He ended by saying he believed Birmingham "was one of the nicer cities as far as the police department is concerned."[26]

Even Siniard had supporters; one of Siniard's fellow church members came to his defense. The person had listened to citizens castigate him and Lynch on *The People Speak* radio broadcast on December 28. The writer penned a letter the next day to Morgan and Bradley, saying they had known the Siniard family for fifteen years, and that "[Siniard] and his wife and children go to the same church that I do and there isn't a finer family nor a more loyal one to the Sunday school and church." The writer thanked Morgan and Bradley for their leniency and for giving Siniard a "second chance." It was curious that they refused to expose their identity, simply closing the letter: "A Member of Fairview Methodist Church."[27]

Siniard had another staunch supporter. In her letter to Mayor Morgan, Mrs. Siniard began by thanking the mayor for giving her "husband back his job." She said he liked being a policeman, adding, "for a person to enjoy his work is very important." Mrs. Siniard acknowledged the enormous publicity about the decision to reinstate her husband, but believed that if "the newspapers and the public knew all the facts, they would be more inclined to agree with you."[28] She continued: "My husband is a good Christian man. He attends Sunday school and church with me and our three children every Sunday. He has always been a good husband and father, and has never been in any trouble before. Please accept my appreciation for what you have done."[29]

The man who had admitted being an accomplice in the assault on my father was a churchgoing Methodist. Birmingham Library Archives Department director Jim Baggett heightened my surprise by remarking that Police Commissioner Eugene "Bull" Connor once taught Sunday school.[30]

The Methodist church in Birmingham had split over segregation and race. The Highlands Methodist Church, of which Ruth Lawson Hanson (wife of the *Birmingham News* publisher) was a member, became the nerve center for laymen resistance to desegregation within the church. The laymen formed the Association of Methodist Ministers and Laymen, and opposed the Council of Methodist Bishops, who had supported the *Brown v. Board of Education* decision. According to historian Glenn T. Eskew, the Birmingham Methodist Ministers Association "renounced the [laymen] movement" because they believed it would "encourage prejudice and hatred."[31]

For many whites in 1954 Birmingham, Christianity was a mere label. The goal of becoming Christlike eluded them.[32]

In her letter to Mayor Morgan, Mrs. A. S. Davis wrote that she had held the mayor in high esteem, believing him to be "a Christian gentleman," but after seeing the way he voted to reinstate Lynch and Siniard after they were fired for the beating, she recanted. "Now I wonder if I know you at all . . . To know that you are a party to such a miscarriage of justice is regrettable."[33]

Quoting an African-American critic in his Auburn University dissertation, Glenn Alan Feldman wrote, the "white Christian church is so suave in its pretense of the practice of Christianity when it comes to the race question that it is practically impotent . . . [It] has stood in the way with a type of deception that is little short of astounding."[34]

My father recalled a sermon he heard on a radio station in Birmingham decades ago. He said the preacher blurted, "I got a soul, you got a soul, a dog got a soul, even a Nigger got a soul." Stoically, Dad added, "That's the way they thought about Negroes at that time."

A shocking incident Feldman discussed in his dissertation involved an Assembly of God minister who at a Ku Klux Klan rally "removed his hood to pray over the victims before they were beaten." Equally as appalling was a reverend's closing prayer at a Birmingham Klan rally: "Heavenly Father, we're grateful we're white."[35]

Several years later, Dr. Martin Luther King Jr. addressed the apathy of the white clergy from the infamous Birmingham jail. King, in lamenting the "laxity of the church," wrote, "I have looked at the South's beautiful churches with their lofty spires pointing heavenward . . . Over and over I have found myself asking: 'What kind of people worship here? Who is their God?'"[36]

Yet amid both indifference and avid support, Birmingham attorney Malcolm Wheeler, who though part of a white culture that was paternalistic toward blacks at best, boldly defended a black man before racist, segregationist powers. In so doing, Wheeler, a Methodist himself, made a mockery of Methodists like Officer Siniard.[37]

Wheeler's integrity, as demonstrated by his prosecution of Lynch and

Siniard on behalf of my father, stands in contrast to the Methodist laymen associations of his day. Another of Wheeler's contemporaries, McClellan "Ted" Van der Veer, of the *Birmingham News,* shared an important relationship with him. Both were affiliated with Wilson Chapel Methodist Church in Roebuck. Van der Veer, also emerged as a major force in the drama surrounding the Patrick case.

I encountered the Wilson Chapel–Van der Veer connection while reading *Birmingham News* columnist James Saxon Childers's account of his first meeting with Van der Veer. Childers was writing a book in Wilson Chapel when "a man on a large black horse rode up." The man was McClellan Van der Veer; he invited Childers to accompany him and his brother for a horseback ride.[38]

Van der Veer, a veteran journalist, once co-owned and published the *Enid Daily News* (Oklahoma) and reported for the *Kansas City Journal, New York Evening Post, New Orleans Item* and *Lexington Kentucky Herald.* He became chief editorial writer for both the *Birmingham News* and *Birmingham Age-Herald* in 1943, and later the editorial page editor of the *News.* In 1955, he was named editor of the *News* until 1960 when he retired.[39]

According to his daughter, Virginia Van der Veer Hamilton, professor of history emerita, the University of Alabama at Birmingham, *News* publisher Clarence Hanson afforded Van der Veer and news side editor-in-chief Charles A. Fell extensive freedom to run their sections. Indeed, many of the front-page news stories about my father's case ran above the fold. Those would have been Fell's decisions. As for the opinion pieces, Van der Veer made the calls.[40]

Hamilton wrote of her father, "he was philosophic, a deep thinker, devoted to peace and brotherhood, and a believer in God."[41]

No editorial that appeared in the *Birmingham News* during that time would have appeared "unless he himself approved what that editorial said," Hamilton explained. Concerning the editorial, "Thirty-day suspension is inadequate in police beating of prisoner," Hamilton concluded that E. L. "Red" Holland, one of her father's assistants, who eventually succeeded him in 1960, wrote it because it lacked her father's "philosophical tone" and was "more practical in its opinion."[42]

"Undoubtedly my father knew of what happened to your father and strongly objected to such police brutality," Hamilton wrote in a 2003 letter to me. "Therefore he allowed his assistant editorial writer to express the opinion of the *News* that the lenient treatment of the officers who were guilty of this act did not fit their crime."[43]

"Clarence Hanson was very conservative," she continued. "It is remarkable that my father was able to express an opinion such as this . . . My father had the highest morals of any man I ever knew," Hamilton said. "He frequently told me: 'No one can corrupt me but myself.'"[44]

Unfortunately, after Van der Veer's retirement in 1960, the *Birmingham News* changed from a progressive newspaper to a "champion of the status quo, even in race relations."[45]

Whether the editorials drove the news coverage or vice versa, yet another person had surfaced who was in a position to positively affect my father's case.

Charles Patrick never met Van der Veer, but he was thankful for the invisible hands that ensured citizen letters and editorials demanding justice on his behalf were published. He remained aware of and thankful for all the citizens, organizations and journalists who kept his case alive.

"I was surprised because white and colored got together and started helping me," Dad said. He recalled how many citizens voiced their opposition to the officers' reinstatement on *The People Speak* radio program.

"The media had a lot to do with it," he said.

The editorials and letters I read in support of my father changed my views about Birmingham. Growing up in Los Angeles, I understood that Birmingham was home to historical civil rights protests. Unfortunately, I had also adopted beliefs that white Americans in the South would forever harbor animus toward African-Americans, that white citizens applauded and embraced violence against blacks, and that white citizens in the South would never change.

But after reading the letters written in response to my father's case, I realized Birmingham was a mixture of nobility and treachery like any other city.

There were moderates and progressives, some of whom were segregationists yet did not espouse violence, but desired fair treatment for blacks; and others who espoused neither segregation nor violence, but felt blacks deserved fairness and equal treatment in all respects. There were also staunch supremacists who upheld segregation and violence against blacks.

I said before that the African-American community in Birmingham valued education, civic duty, discipline and church. The anomaly is that white Southerners shared many of these same values. Yet prejudice and racism restricted, even canceled the ability of a large number to express civility, rendering them incapable of embracing their fellow black citizens. Still, there was enough humanity, enough courage left in some to support Charles Patrick. Over the mistreatment of one black man, many whites unashamedly cried foul.[46]

For certain, the relentless citizen letters, coupled with the efforts of Commissioner Lindbergh, Chief Pattie, attorney Malcolm Wheeler and a formidable Birmingham press churning out dozens of front-page news articles were factors that kept Charles Patrick buoyed and motivated to press on.

6
The Wheel Stops Turning

Some people can tolerate oppression as long as the oppressor does not get too personal.

On numerous occasions my father said he was content to stay in his place and raise his family. He did not seek to arouse the ire of Southern terrorists lusting for an uppity Negro to abuse. But when white oppressors singled him out, it was on.

Immediately after Mayor Morgan and Commissioner Bradley voted to reinstate the officers who had assaulted him, Dad asked Malcolm Wheeler to file state and federal charges in addition to a civil damage suit against them.

Wheeler first filed a petition for a rehearing because he found two volunteer witnesses who corroborated Dad's version of the confrontation with Mrs. Lynch. Wheeler openly declared that the beating was "clearly a federal offense." He told police reporter Bill Mobley, "…plenty is going to happen since the city commission has seen fit to reinstate two officers who have admitted violating federal, state and county laws."[1]

Politicians are known to do two things when they encounter public disapproval: defend and justify.

Morgan told the press at city hall that he "probably would not reverse his decision" to suspend Lynch and Siniard, claiming Lindbergh and Pattie failed to make a case for dismissing them from the police force.

He also said he believed he had tempered "justice with mercy," and that the thirty-day suspension was a stiff enough penalty.[2]

John Temple Graves had called for a reopening of the Patrick case in his column. He got it.

Judge Parker attracted onlookers to Recorder's Court when he reopened my father's case on December 30, 1954. Parker listened to the witnesses Wheeler brought in to testify that my father did not curse at Mrs. Lynch, a major point of contention in the case. Fred L. Calhoun, a black school teacher, told the judge he had heard the entire confrontation and that no profanity was uttered. He said he gave his name to Detective W. M. Prier at the scene of the incident, but Prier told Calhoun "he was too far away to hear anything." Assistant City Attorney Charles Brown never called Calhoun to testify at the first trial on December 17.[3]

Another witness, Robert V. Ryder, a white contractor who had been standing nearby, said he heard no profanity and "didn't see Patrick shake the door handle of Mrs. Lynch's car," as she had testified. He also said, "Patrick drove away after a few seconds and let Mrs. Lynch have the parking place."[4]

According to news reports, Parker ordered my father to submit to a lie detector test.

"I didn't know what a lie detector test was, but I would do anything to clear my name," Dad said.

On December 31, within days of Parker's directive, two front-page headlines on both the *Birmingham News* and *Post-Herald* announced the lie detector test. A photograph of my father ran with the story published in the *News*. Dad said it was the first time he recalled ever seeing a photo of a black man on the cover of a white-owned Birmingham newspaper.

Parker's request for a lie detector test caused an instant and negative reaction.

"We're trying to build up the lie detector as an investigative aid—not as an aid to prosecute anyone in court," protested Police Chief Pattie.[5]

My father was the third person Parker had ever ordered to take the test, a test he said helped him arrive at the truth. "I cannot administer justice fairly if I cannot ascertain the truth," Parker said.[6]

But Pattie's argument was that "if there's reasonable doubt in the judge's mind, the defendant should go free." He also explained that state law prohibited the results of the test being used in court. He added, "When the evidence is put up in court, that's it. If the police department hasn't made an adequate investigation in the judge's opinion, the defendant should go free."[7]

The *Birmingham News* cautioned against overdependence on the tests in its January 7 editorial. In commenting on the rift between Parker and Pattie, the paper pointed out that the FBI "makes no use of lie detectors . . . and Director Edgar Hoover questions their value." Nevertheless, the paper stated its reluctance to oppose the use of the lie detector in my father's case because "the power of a judge to go beyond the evidence submitted to him and to use the functions of the court to get whatever additional evidence he thinks desirable is, and should be, broad."[8]

Parker got what he wanted. Captain Glenn V. Evans, the only department official who knew how to operate the polygraph machine at the time, was charged with administering the test on a piece of equipment that was twelve years old, and "badly in need of repairs."[9]

Howell Raines interviewed Evans for his book *My Soul Is Rested,* and described him as "deeply religious." According to Raines, a spiritual conversion precipitated Evans's loss of faith in Eugene "Bull" Connor and in segregation.[10]

"I suspect that Evans's fair handling of your father's lie detector test was part of the process by which he overcame his racism, which I believe he did to a remarkable degree for a man of his time and profession," Raines explained. "It is hard to imagine another white police officer [in] Birmingham at that time who would have had the courage to say your father was not lying. It's quite striking really that in that brutal time a man of your father's courage and a man with Evans's sense of fair play would find their paths crossing."[11]

Judge Parker continued to defend his use of the tests. He told reporters that of the one hundred thousand cases he had tried, in only three had he requested lie detector tests. He acknowledged that though "the weight of the evidence" appeared to be in "Patrick's favor," he reportedly "wanted all the weight he could muster in the case."[12]

Meanwhile, Wheeler was in the midst of a propaganda war with James G. Adams, counsel for officers Lynch and Siniard. It appeared Adams was trying to sway my father against ending his clients' careers, for Dad had not yet filed charges before the Jefferson County Civil Service Personnel Board.

Both attorneys were using the news media to their advantage. And while they did not exactly stoop to trying their cases in the press, neither Wheeler nor Adams was shy about firing off pithy quotes to reporters.

Adams once told the press my father informed him "he had forgiven the policemen for the beating 'because I did not want those men with families to lose their jobs.'" Wheeler countered, again declaring that Patrick had "advised me to prosecute the two policemen through the state and federal channels, plus a civil-damage suit for assault and battery."[13]

Adams, ever wily and manipulative, once tried flattery to dissuade my father from pursuing his clients. He told an African-American reporter from the *Birmingham World,* "That man, Charles Patrick, is an upright, understanding gentleman and Christian man." Then Adams tried to elicit sympathy by attempting to explain why Lynch had beaten him. "Any human being is subject to become upset when he feels that he or someone close to him has been offended. And Patrick understands that."[14]

My father told me that at no time did he intend to let the officers off the hook. He wanted them fired and sent to prison because they had committed a crime.

The *Birmingham World,* which had captured Wheeler's and Adams's verbal jousts, also reported that the FBI had completed its investigation of possible civil rights violations, though the FBI had yet to report its findings or return indictments. And the *World* attributed no source to its report. Up to that time, the federal agency had been mysteriously silent.[15]

Meanwhile, my father was readying for another assault on Lynch and Siniard. A thirty-day suspension was not enough; Dad wanted them fired. So on January 5, 1955, a few days before he was to take the lie detector test, Dad visited with Personnel Board Director Ray Mullins. After his meeting, he told reporters he discussed with Mullins the possibility of filing charges against the officers, but wanted first to "talk with Malcolm Wheeler."[16]

Though I inquired, my father refused to divulge what he and Wheeler discussed, but the outcome was telling, for the next day, January 6, Dad filed charges against Lynch and Siniard. Alone.

Mullins told the personnel board "that Malcolm Wheeler, who represented Patrick in city court, was not representing him in this case." For certain my father had intended to represent himself because according to board minutes, he had advised members "he would not be able to obtain legal assistance in prosecuting the charges." Thus Mullins's planned to "render the complainant . . . whatever assistance might be necessary in order to bring out all the facts in the case."[17]

In an effort to address the unusual act of a black man filing charges against white police officers, alone and without counsel, Board Chairman Howard Yielding said, "Every citizen has the right to file charges before this board. I act on the premise that nobody ought to have to have counsel to appear before this board." Indeed, my father told reporters he was filing the charges "as a citizen and qualified voter." Associate board members Charles A. Long and James F. Sulzby Jr. also served on the board under Mullins and Yielding, director and chairman respectively.[18]

Mullins said he had studied the "facts of the controversial police case enough to believe the Negro was 'justified' in filing charges."[19]

In my father's handwritten complaint, he accused Lynch and Siniard of "beating, kicking and stomping me unmercifully while I was being held a prisoner in the City Jail."[20]

The policemen had five days to respond to the charges, and the board was required to hold a hearing within twenty days thereafter. Lynch and Siniard had much to lose. The board could decide their futures as civil servants.

I asked my father if he feared retaliation from Klansmen or the officers' friends during that time. He said no. He believed God was "keeping them [hostile white citizens] away . . . They wouldn't touch me with a ten-foot pole."

I do not think I grasped the depth of my father's resolve until I read that he went alone and filed handwritten charges against his assailants. It altered my understanding of the civil rights movement in Birmingham. All I had ever read and seen were African-Americans marching in groups, peacefully protesting various injustices with Dr. Martin Luther King Jr., Fred Shuttlesworth, Ralph Abernathy or others at the forefront.

But here was my father, first with and then without an attorney, pursuing corrupt cops. I also learned of others besides Dad unafraid to take a stand, alone.

Youths like Dr. Horace Huntley, who harassed white bus drivers and threw rocks at KKK processions in Birmingham. Men like Marine Timothy Hood, who in the 1940s moved the color bar on a streetcar, fought with the conductor and lost his life in the process, prompting a protest march of 1,200 people in Bessemer. Army Pfc. Thomas Edwards Brooks, who in 1950 refused orders to board a Montgomery bus from the rear, shoved the bus driver and a policeman, and was shot dead after he bolted. Unnamed black women in Alabama, who fought with bus passengers and streetcar operators rather than submit to Jim Crow segregation laws. The eighty-eight incidents where blacks took bus and streetcar seats designated for white passengers in 1942 underscored the historical courage of the South's African-American population, long before Rosa Parks's brave stand on a Montgomery bus in December 1955.[21]

Strangely, my father did not even have civil rights in mind as he went about planning his next moves. I once posed the question: So you weren't taking a stand for black people?

"No," he replied. "I was thinking about raising my family. I wasn't thinking about black history."

My father's determination to raise his family and stay in his place was inconsistent with his fierce pursuit of Lynch and Siniard. But the explanation was simple: They picked the fight. Lynch and Siniard were only doing what policemen had been allowed to do to black people in Birmingham. Nonetheless, their violent meddling was about to result in acute humbling.

The day arrived for Dad to take the lie detector test. Evans administered three separate tests to my father on January 7, each consisting of ten to twelve questions, conducted in a private room. A few posed were: "Did you in any way act disorderly at the scene? Did you curse Mrs. Lynch? Did you go to the door of Mrs. Lynch's car? Did you curse in the presence or hearing of Mrs. Lynch?"[22]

Dad answered no to all. Evans said it would take about three days before he would know the results.[23]

As Evans pored over test results, my mother was at home busily clipping and cataloguing newspaper articles, editorials and citizen letters in Dad's scrapbook. In fact, she got so carried away that she sometimes clipped off publication names and dates. One intriguing article discussed the Greater Birmingham Emancipation Association's denunciation of police brutality in the Patrick case, but it was impossible for me to render proper attribution.

As days passed, reporters from the *News, Post-Herald* and *World* kept the case alive with prominent placement on their front pages. The *World* announced a "gigantic mass meeting" scheduled for Sunday, January 16, 1955, at Sixteenth Street Baptist Church. Sponsored by the Birmingham branch of the NAACP, the meeting kept residents abreast of developments with the case.[24]

Officer Siniard was the first to respond to Personnel Board charges. On January 11, through his attorney, C. E. Huey, Siniard denied "each and every count," and said, "any further disciplinary action against [me] is not warranted." Lynch, who was represented by James Adams, must have responded soon thereafter because the officers' hearing was set for January 26, 1955.[25]

It became clear why Malcolm Wheeler was not present when my father appeared before the personnel board. On January 13, Dad filed more charges through famed civil rights attorneys Orzell Billingsley Jr. and Peter A. Hall Sr., both of whom worked with the legendary Arthur Shores. This time Jackson was the target with Billingsley and Hall citing Jackson for taking Lynch and Siniard to Patrick's jail cell, failing to report the incident and failing to provide my father with medical care. Hall and Billingsley also added additional charges against Lynch and Siniard for initially testifying "falsely under oath." Jackson's hearing was also set for January 26.[26]

Apparently, during my father's discussion with Wheeler prior to appearing before the board, they must have come to an agreement that Wheeler would no longer represent him. Their parting, however, was not the result of a disagreement over money because my father had said fees for Wheeler's legal services came from Mason collections at black churches and NAACP fund-raisers.[27]

It was simply that Wheeler had made his purposes clear the day Judge Parker reopened the case on December 30: "'to clear my client's [Patrick's] name' and get the vagrancy charges against him nol-prossed [cleared off the books]." Dad's additional charges against the officers were beyond the scope of Wheeler's stated aim. Perhaps he had made it clear to my father that if he could win an acquittal, he was out. Whatever happened, Dad said there was no argument or disagreement between him and Wheeler. The latter had simply committed to getting my father's name cleared, and he did.[28]

However, neither would wait long to see if their efforts together had paid off. Front page, January 14, 1955, *Birmingham Post-Herald:* "In Jail Beating Case, Patrick Acquitted of Being Disorderly." Mission accomplished.

The acquittal was based on Evans's testimony that my father had passed the lie detector test. Evans testified, "No reaction from the defendant indicated that he was telling a lie. In my opinion, he was telling the truth."[29]

Though still physically recovering from the beating, Dad's sense of dignity had been restored.

On a sunny day in Los Angeles, May 23, 2002, my father beamed and exhaled as he read the above newspaper article announcing his acquittal.

"Let the record so state. And that's it," he declared.

Enough. I closed my reporter's notebook and stopped the tape.

7

Attorney Tango

A Lively Shuffle

The plan changed. At first, my father merely wanted to clear his name. He had often said so. That was probably the reason Malcolm Wheeler once told the press his client was "content to let the matter drop as long as the men were dismissed from the department."[1]

But the thought that officers Lynch and Siniard deserved just punishment for their crime continued to trouble him. It came out during our interviews. What consumed him was: 1) The officers beat him while wearing weapons. 2) He kept pleading, "This is wrong!" as they hit, stomped and kicked him.

It was the unfairness of it. Lynch and Siniard had to pay. And for justice, Dad said he was willing to die. However, he did drop the idea of filing a civil suit for monetary damages.

"I didn't ask for anything from them whatsoever. I would work to make my living. My strength did come back," he said.

The worst for a writer is encountering dueling sources, especially when those sources are one's parents. My mother told me Dad's case was first given to premier civil rights attorney Arthur Shores and that he passed it on to Orzell Billingsley Jr. Dad said not so, though he could not recall how he met Billingsley and Peter A. Hall Sr., except to say that they were NAACP attorneys.

The reputations of the attorneys who represented my father were enough to raise the profile of his case. They were the black intellectuals of that era, the elites.

Billingsley and Hall practiced law with Shores in 1954; their address at 1630 Fourth Avenue North was well-known as the Masonic Temple building. All three men represented Dr. Martin Luther King Jr. in later years. Most notably, Shores was part of the legal team that had worked with Thurgood Marshall, who later became the first African-American to serve on the U.S. Supreme Court, in the historical *Brown v. Board of Education* ruling.[2]

It was unapologetic competence that characterized their approach. As Alabama counsel for the NAACP Inc. Fund, Shores once told historian Howell Raines:

"It was amusing for us to go into courts where these white lawyers were really unprepared . . . and I mean it was ludicrous to see some of these so-called white constitutional lawyers get up and just flail the wind. See, they had been used to their political . . . state courts. They really hadn't been used to practicing too much in federal courts, and civil rights was unheard of, so far as their having to prepare for or against it. And they were not prepared and none of these cases were lost."[3]

Dickson used the word "fearless" in describing both Hall and Billingsley. "Orzell was a little more gung ho, more militant," he said. "Orzell was a wild guy. You either liked him or you didn't like him."[4]

Peter Hall Jr., Birmingham Municipal Court principal magistrate, distinctly remembers visiting the law offices where his father, Billingsley and Shores practiced. He definitely cannot forget Billingsley.

"He always seemed to have a joyful and up-tempo attitude and personality," Hall said. "There always seemed to be laughter when he came to our home."[5]

According to Dickson, who looked after Billingsley until his death in

2001, Billingsley was a hardworking man, handling cases sometimes for free and quoting poetry on a whim "that had a reference to what you were doing." After the Patrick case ended, when he was not representing the likes of Dr. King or Shuttlesworth, he was receiving calls from President John F. Kennedy and later President Lyndon Johnson, or traveling around Alabama incorporating small black majority towns—twenty, according to the Congressional Record.[6]

After his wife died, things changed. Billingsley, who was a veteran, became difficult to deal with, did not answer his phone and was noticeably detached. Yet one could find him in his office in the afternoons. "He went to pieces . . . didn't care about anything," Dickson said.[7]

Hall Sr., on the other hand, was conservative, well-dressed, religious, an elder in the Presbyterian Church. Like Billingsley, he served in the military.

Hall Sr. and his son talked frequently about old civil rights issues from the 1950s, 1960s and 1970s, as well as more current issues from 1980–1986. "But mainly current issues," Hall Jr. said. He added that his father also discussed his participation on different boards and committees such as Operation New Birmingham, NAACP, Birmingham Bar Association, Alpha Phi Alpha Fraternity, Miller Memorial Presbyterian Church and others.[8]

"He frequently expressed his willingness and desire to work with the white community for the betterment of Birmingham," he said of his father.[9]

Hall Sr. eventually became a municipal judge, a book judge who required the prosecution to prove their case beyond a reasonable doubt. And while he might make attorneys wait as late as 10 p.m., Judge Hall was known to give fair trials and would turn defendants loose if a prosecutor failed to make the case.[10]

"You knew when you went in Peter Hall's court that you had to be disciplined . . . He had to set the standards and he proved and showed that he was going to make a difference," Dickson said. "He had this reputation that when you went in Peter Hall's court that Peter didn't play."[11]

Photographs of Billingsley, Hall and Shores reveal debonair men who not only dressed well, but knew how to sport that *look*. In headshots I obtained, none were grinning, but all exuded a no-nonsense savvy, their collective intuitive gazes asking, "Are you prepared to do battle with us in court?"

Indeed, Hall Jr. said his father and colleagues often met in the home of Adene "Deanie" Drew, wife of an insurance agency owner, to "talk strategy."[12]

Hall and Billingsley were as comfortable trying cases in the U.S. Supreme Court as they were in Birmingham's Recorder's Court. A few Supreme Court cases in which they were involved include *Reeves v. Alabama, Hamilton v. Alabama, Fikes v. Alabama* and *Shuttlesworth v. Birmingham*. Birmingham attorney Mason Davis knew Hall and Billingsley well, having partnered with them at the firm Hall, Billingsley and Davis. He said Shores also argued many cases before the Supreme Court, one of which was a landmark employment discrimination case involving the railroads.[13]

Though uncommon for that era, Dad's case—whereby white policemen were prosecuted for assaulting a black man—was not a first. Before an all-white jury, Shores prosecuted a white policeman for assaulting a black union leader in 1940—and won.[14]

Historian William A. Nunnelley described attorneys of Shores's, Billingsley's and Hall's caliber as members of the "black upper class," who were "offended" by confrontational tactics that came to be associated with the civil rights movement in later years. These elites "opposed the use of direct action."[15]

They preferred instead to outthink opponents in courtroom arenas, attacking, abolishing, altering or creating new laws—at the federal level, if necessary. And they were not opposed to seeking public office, as in the cases of Shores and Hall, to induce change from within.

That is not to say Hall and Billingsley did not interact with civil rights activist groups. Both men served on the NAACP's executive committee; and the organization openly supported my father, having passed a resolution deploring the beating.[16]

Though Charles Patrick did not consider himself a member of the "black upper class," he shared in common with Hall and Billingsley military service and a preference for decisive legal maneuvers, as well as solid moral values: integrity, honesty, hard work, patriotism. And like his two attorneys, Dad was not one to lock arms and march in large groups, though he did approve of the nonviolent public faceoffs with the racist establishment and of the mass resistance that emerged after his trial. Yet both styles were needed to wrestle the forces that controlled Birmingham during that era.

Charles Patrick's acquittal of disorderly conduct charges on January 13 must have been good news for Hall and Billingsley, who were preparing to appear before the Jefferson County Civil Service Personnel Board on January 26, 1955, to argue for the dismissal of Lynch, Siniard and Jackson.

The press did not reduce coverage about the Patrick case as long as new details emerged. *Jet* magazine ran an update in its January 13, 1955, weekly edition, keeping the case in national focus. The *Chicago Defender* ran two news briefs in its January 8, 1955, national edition. The *Birmingham News* published that officers Lynch and Siniard had returned to work the week of January 16. Deputy Warden Jackson was already back in uniform by the time the article ran. And a continuing flow of negative publicity about Birmingham's police department could only have helped the Patrick case. In mid-January, Judge Robert J. Wheeler denied probation to Birmingham police officer Robert Slaughter after the officer pled guilty to grand larceny.[17]

While the white press was at work, the black community was making news of its own. During the early stages of his trial, my father pursued the officers alone by means of one white attorney, and with the moral support of family, neighbors, churches and friends at ACIPCO. Churches and organizations constructed a cocoon of support around Charles and Rutha Patrick and their five children.

It was difficult for the family during the days my father was unable to work. Dad said he had tried to return to ACIPCO, but could not due to the injuries he had sustained. My mother, nine months pregnant in January 1955, said she was working part-time at Pizitz department store when the officers assaulted my father. A neighborhood girl kept my siblings while she worked. With the baby's due date looming, money was a major concern.

Often when my father spoke of the financial effects the case had on the family, his speech slowed, tone softened, gaze shifted downward.

"That's where the churches and the Masons came in to help me, and they raised money for me to pay my bills and stop the foreclosure on my [Washington Heights] home," he explained. "It was a NAACP meeting and all the churches were bringing money in there."

My parents were dedicated members of Harmony Street Baptist Church. Their pastor, Reverend M. W. Whitt, took a lead role in helping heighten community support for my father. The NAACP held at least three mass meetings in January 1955 at Sixteenth Street Baptist Church. Whitt addressed attendees at one of the rallies; my father remembered speaking at two. And though Hall and Billingsley also attended, my father said they did not speak.

These gatherings also doubled as fund-raisers for both the organization and my father. One church channeled its collections directly to him, bypassing the NAACP.

I found a short memo in the family scrapbook on Sardis Baptist Church letterhead, Reverend R. L. Alford presiding. The January 16, 1955, memo, its edges now yellow and delicate, simply stated, "The pastor and members of the Sardis Baptist Church present to Mr. Charles Patrick the sum of $51.70."[18]

The family scrapbook was a treasure. My mother, a meticulous record keeper, wrote down the names of each church and individual who donated money, including the amount most times. More than one amount was scribbled next to certain churches. Harmony Street Baptist Church topped the list, followed by Bethel Baptist, Miller Memorial Presbyterian, St. Mark Baptist, Groveland, First Baptist Church Hooper City, Mount Tabor, Mount Olive, Zion Springs, First Baptist Woodlawn and Mount Hebron Baptist Churches. The list also included individuals and pastors. On that list, I counted more than $600 in donations to my parents, money that went for food, the mortgage and other family needs.

"They wanted to put me outdoors, but the churches paid all of that up," Dad said.

Record keeping was not the only way my mother supported Dad: "Momma just prayed for me that everything would be all right for me," my father once said. "I had a family I knew would stick behind me."

As the date neared for the face-off before the personnel board, so did my mother's showdown in the delivery room of South Highland Hospital.

Black women were kept in the basement of the hospital until moments before delivery, then rushed up via the elevator to give birth before being hurried right back down to recuperate. My mother was in the basement when labor indicated it was time to go.

"If the black woman started to deliver in the elevator, they'd [hospital staff] hold her legs together," my mother said.

That's what happened to her, only the baby turned completely around, so Mom was taken back down to the basement. Had the hospital been more hospitable to women of color, they might have saved my mother twenty-four hours of additional agony. Fortunately, "an old white doctor from ACIPCO" gave her a shot of glucose, she said.

"Marydeane kicked, and I delivered her in the basement . . . without anesthesia that I can recall," Mom said.

My father had little time to celebrate Marydeane's birth with his wife of eight years. It was an exhausting time for both of them. My grand-mother kept my other siblings while my mother remained in the hospital four or five days.

Marydeane was born one day before the fates of the men who had nearly killed her father were to be decided.

Malcolm Wheeler had dealt the first blow. Peter Hall and Orzell Billingsley prepared for the knockout.

8

Battle of the Board

If attorneys Orzell Billingsley Jr. and Peter A. Hall Sr. were the infantry, then Birmingham's press was heavy artillery. And as though softening the enemy's resolve, John Temple Graves lobbed another one via his *Post-Herald* column. "Policemen can beat up a Negro prisoner in Birmingham's jail, let the world be told, but, by all the gods, policemen can't get away with it. Their fellow policemen won't stand for it, Chief Pattie won't, Commissioner Lindbergh won't, the personnel board won't, and we the people won't."[1]

Pre-publicity for a controversial court case is like a movie trailer. It teases, tantalizes and invites onlookers to care, react—anything but remain indifferent.

Graves, like attorney Malcolm Wheeler and editor McClellan Van der Veer, was affiliated with Wilson Chapel Methodist Church, and did much to keep public opinion stirred. His column reflected the collective conscience of the part of the white community that was outraged by the treatment of Patrick. With former Police Commissioner Eugene "Bull" Connor out, it was their time: a four-year period when moderate, racially progressive powers spoke, however cautiously.

The *Birmingham News* published a news brief reminding readers of the January 26, 1955, personnel board hearing. It recapped the charges

Patrick filed against Lynch, Siniard and Jackson.[2] On January 24, the city commission held its pre-commission session. The pending Patrick case invited more attention to the routine weekly gathering with reporters showing up from three competing newspapers.[3] An innocent occurrence, yet when tension and anxiety envelope a trial, the smallest events become major.

On the day of the hearing, January 26, the personnel board raised the question as to whether pre-commission sessions were really public meetings. Why that issue was even thought worthy of consideration is baffling. But while ruling on a matter that was discussed at the January 24 city commission pre-session, board chairman Howard Yielding declared such assemblies are not public meetings, prompting defense attorney C. E. Huey to squabble, "Three newspapers were represented and I feel that made it a public hearing."[4]

Certainly everyone was on edge as Charles Patrick recounted the evening of December 11, 1954, when Lynch beat him while Siniard and Jackson held his arms outstretched.

Personnel board members Howard Yielding, James F. Sulzby Jr. and Charles A. Long listened to evidence that began at 5 p.m. and ended at 1 a.m. Though personnel board minutes did not capture verbatim testimony from the hearing, the minutes listed those who testified. Present on behalf of my father were Police Chief Pattie, Assistant Police Chief Moore, Captain Garrison, Assistant Warden for Fingerprinting Leland A. Holcomb, and citizens Jesse Smiley, Eddie Melson and Jim Wilmon. Witnesses supporting officers Lynch, Siniard and Jackson were Reverend S. T. Kimbrough, Detective W. M. Prier, Jack Yauger, W. P. McRee, H. L. Tourney, W. W. Self, J. H. Woolley, Dewey Murchison, A. Payne, C. D. Guy, Joe B. Norman, Richard P. Sandefer and Nelson Weaver.[5]

Those in the fingerprinting room who witnessed the assault were Smiley, a black man, Wilmon, Melson and Holcomb, all white. While my father contended that Siniard hit him, too, none of the witnesses agreed, but they did allege Siniard and Jackson held his arms. All except Melson, who played it safe. He told the board he saw "a sort of commotion down the hall. There was a colored fellow and some officers scuffling around." He added that he did not recognize any of the officers present at the hearing.[6]

The testimony was graphic. "I heard them hollering in the hall . . . two policemen holding his [Patrick's] arms and a big policeman boxing him with his fists . . . one of the officers twisting his left arm behind him . . . They were hitting him on the head . . . The big policeman put his foot on Patrick's head and kicked him five or six times . . . I saw Lynch hit him right in the stomach . . . I saw Lynch stomp Patrick around the neck and shoulders and kick him in the side . . . I saw Officer Lynch swing his fist at Patrick, and a short time later, I saw blood on the floor in the hallway . . . All the time, Patrick was trying to protect his face with his hands."[7]

Perhaps the most self-serving testimony was Jackson's, an active accessory to the crime, who ended up helping the prosecution.

Garrison said Jackson had given a statement previously that he allowed Lynch and Siniard into the cell block and soon "a bunch of licks were passed," but that he "did not strike him [Patrick] at all."[8] Though Jackson held my father's arm, he was credited with stopping the beating after he saw the Masonic distress signal. Dad said the district attorney called Jackson a "nigger lover" for doing so. And the district attorney was not the only one.

"He [Jackson] was afraid because he was telling them that they beat me up—and everyone [supporters of Lynch and Siniard] in the court called him a nigger lover, and I don't know what happened to him," Dad said.

Testimony proving the patrolmen "falsely testified under oath" was given by Garrison and Moore.[9]

Garrison testified that Lynch told him on December 17 that he "had never seen Patrick before nor had he been to the jail on the night of the beating," and that Siniard had said the same thing. Moore effectively painted Lynch a liar when he testified that Lynch later "admitted going to the jail, having Patrick called out and then striking him with his fist."[10]

In an attempt to mitigate this damaging testimony, attorneys Huey and Adams argued the court record did not show that Lynch and Siniard were under oath during the December 17, 1954, Recorder's Court trial. Hall and Billingsley countered by putting Police Chief Pattie on the stand and having him read the police manual whereby all officers are "to speak the truth at all times."[11]

The gyrations proved futile. Board Chairman Howard Yielding silenced all with his assertion that civil service employees are always expected to speak the truth. "That's this board's position; that's this board's attitude and that's this board's policy."[12]

A point of contention was whether the officers beat Patrick while wearing sidearms. My father insisted they did, and in our interviews it remained a major contention of his fifty years later.

In a 2002 interview while explaining why the public reacted so strongly to the beating, Dad said, "Because these people [citizens] did not like what they did, coming to beat me up in jail with their guns on their sides."

There was a frown, a wince, and I instantly knew my father could still see those weapons.

Some witnesses to the beating, however, said they saw holsters only, no sidearms, and other officers said pistols were checked at the jail door. Since some of those making this contention were colleagues of Lynch and Siniard who witnessed the assault, and because they did not stop the attack nor offer aid after the beating, their testimony was suspect.[13]

Up until the January 26 board hearing, the *Birmingham News* assigned no bylines to stories about the Patrick beating. But someone at the paper decided to assign staff reporter Harry Cook to cover the late-night personnel board hearing. Likewise, there were no bylines on *Birmingham World* articles until its January 28 edition when reporter Marcel Hopson's byline appeared.

Both Hopson's and Cook's articles read like the court legal record. Painstakingly meticulous, Hopson actually followed the order of sworn testimony and captured my father's responses to defense attorneys on cross-examinations.

Dad once contended, "I did see Officer Lynch strike me in the face with his fists. I was flat on my back when they were beating me; I was hit repeatedly by Officer Lynch." An article written by managing editor Alford Stone of the *Birmingham Mirror* was also thorough. Yet phrases like "alleged 'unmerciful beating'" "alleged charge," and "supposedly victim of alleged" either underscored the paper's attempt to avoid libel or were designed to invite skepticism. By the time of the personnel board hearing, most reporters were writing as though the beating happened. Unlike other reporters, however, Stone was the only one who disclosed Siniard's previous "unofficial reprimand" from police department superiors. The reason for the reprimand was not disclosed.[14]

The board reconvened the following day, January 27, at 4:30 p.m. to hear closing arguments. The hearing had been delayed at the request of Huey, who was simultaneously engaged in a circuit court trial. The board members were set to issue a ruling in the case, but member James Sulzby had missed ten minutes of testimony the day before so action was delayed for that reason as well.[15]

It was the attorneys' moment—and they milked it.

Adams, representing Lynch, made two motions to toss out my father's complaint "on grounds it was not properly filed" because Lynch was not served with an amendment to the original charges. The second was a charge that citizens did not have the right "to ask the civil service board [to] review . . . a suspension ordered by appointing authorities." Chairman Yielding overruled both. Adams also alleged both officers were off duty and were not wearing weapons or blackjacks "as testified to by

Patrick." He pleaded with board members to "temper your verdict with justice and mercy."[16]

In his closing arguments, Huey, attorney for Siniard and Jackson, argued that Jackson's admitting the two officers to the cell block was a "routine duty" and that at no time had Patrick "asked for medical attention, and, according to testimony, did not appear to be in need of such." He also charged that my father was the only one who accused Siniard of hitting him, and at one time had said "he did not remember being hit by anyone other than Lynch." He also said Jackson "did nothing to get Patrick out of the cell block." While he agreed that Jackson was wrong not to report the incident, he stressed that his ten-day suspension was punishment enough.[17]

Billingsley opened his closing argument with a terse response to Adams: "We have to have justice before we can temper it." In the course of their arguments, Hall and Billingsley relied on the police manual and reminders to the board about an officer's official duty.[18]

"The police manual sets that an officer is not a judge." They went on to charge that Lynch and Siniard made "their own decision of guilt." Hall specifically said the officers were "unworthy" of the title and stressed, "As guardians of the life and property and well-being of citizens, it is their duty to protect them from harm."[19]

Hall and Billingsley used the schoolmaster approach to remind the personnel board that it was their "duty to see to it that those men entrusted with a badge and pistol are guardians and protectors of the people . . . These men have done a thing which the board cannot ignore."[20]

In addition to pointing out that no witnesses said the beating did not happen, Billingsley reminded them "the only issue before the board was whether Patrick had been beaten."[21]

With that, board members closed the hearing Friday afternoon and began deliberating.

On January 29, the front pages of the *Post-Herald* and *News* announced the verdict: the dismissal of officers Lynch and Siniard from the

Birmingham Police Department. The *World* announced the same three days later on February 1.[22]

Immediately after the Friday decision, Police Chief Pattie called Lynch and Siniard to his office and "stripped them of their badges." Pattie dismissed the officers "in the middle of . . . [the] evening shift."[23]

In its written opinion and decision letter, the board ruled that all three defendants were "guilty as charged," however, Jackson's ten-day suspension was deemed adequate. And while Lynch could never work a civil service job in Birmingham again, the board left an avenue open for Siniard to work in other civil service positions for which he might be qualified.[24]

However, reporters quickly determined that Siniard was ineligible to become a Birmingham policeman because of his age. Siniard had already turned thirty-five; persons over thirty-four were barred.[25]

Personnel board members praised attorneys Billingsley and Hall at the end of the two-day hearing, but only the black-owned *Birmingham World* published the comments. Board Chairman Yielding and members Sulzby and Long together commended the attorneys for "the superb manner in which they presented their case, and, above all, their conduct."[26]

The national press continued covering the case. *Jet* magazine's February 17, 1955, edition announced the personnel board's decision to fire officers Lynch and Siniard, as did the *Chicago Defender*'s February 12, 1955, edition. Detailed reports written by *Post-Herald*'s Andrew Glaze and *News* reporter Harry Cook prompted another round of newspaper editorials and citizen letters.

In its January 31 edition, a *Post-Herald* editorial lauded the personnel board's action: "Firing the two officers involved was the only course that could be taken consistent with right and civic honor." It also encouraged citizens to recall that Commissioner Lindbergh had fired the officers initially.

Birmingham citizen N. Gresham Early sent a letter published February 3 to the *Birmingham News* in which he taunted Mayor Morgan and Commissioner Bradley, questioning how they must feel after being overruled by the board.

Morgan did not stick around long to read it. He left for New York after the ruling, and Bradley checked himself into a hospital "for a minor operation." Only Commissioner Lindbergh was at his city hall office. As a result, the February 1 city commission meeting was canceled for lack of a quorum.[27]

The historic decision to terminate two Birmingham officers as a result of a black man's accusations scored high on the civic Richter scale. Change was the word.

Pattie announced major personnel shuffling in the police department. He placed Captain J. C. Lance over the Uniformed Patrol Division and Captain J. W. Haley over the Criminal Investigation Division. Both assignments became effective February 1, 1955. Finally, at the request of Pattie, the personnel board increased the minimum age for patrolmen from twenty to twenty-three. The maximum age remained thirty-four.[28]

A call for new officers was announced in the February 15 edition of the *News*. Examinations for new patrolmen aged twenty-three and above were scheduled for March 11. And Morgan and Pattie announced plans to hire policewomen for the force in the "near future," an extraordinary step for Birmingham at that time.[29]

There was a good reason the department needed as many female and male officers as they could get. Years of official misconduct and outright criminality on the force had taken its toll. Officer dismissals ran high. The Birmingham Police Department had become a victim of its own vices. From 1953 to 1955, dozens of police officers had been disciplined or relieved of duty for armed robbery, theft, grand larceny, fighting and burglary.[30]

No doubt the slew of embarrassing violations left the rank and file demoralized, so Pattie took the bold step of holding confidential meetings with every member in his department. He wanted to give officers and other personnel an opportunity to "get it off the chest." Though admitting the sessions would be time consuming, he said he wanted "everybody to have a chance to express himself."[31]

As Pattie was tending to his rank and file, Lynch was fighting back. First, he filed notice to appeal the personnel board's decision immediately after his firing, then months later in September 1955 he sued the NAACP for $100,000. Filed through Lynch's new attorney, Robert N. Pratt, the suit claimed several members of the NAACP persuaded "Charles Patrick . . . to press charges against him, resulting in the loss of his job." Named in the suit were attorneys Hall and Billingsley, *Birmingham World* managing editor Emory Jackson and NAACP southeast regional secretary Ruby Hurley, among others. Lynch claimed that since NAACP attorneys represented Patrick, the defendants did not have a right to "aid or abet, or help pay for the prosecution."[32]

Billingsley and Hall prepared to file a motion of their own. The former announced to the *Birmingham World* plans to soon file "federal charges of civil rights violation" against Lynch, Siniard and Jackson on behalf of Patrick.[33]

The FBI's clandestine investigation had gone public during the personnel board's testimony. The *Post-Herald* and *News* reported the Bureau had completed its findings on whether my father's civil rights had been violated and had sent them to the Department of Justice in Washington, D.C.[34]

With federal indictments looming, Lynch, Siniard and Jackson no doubt wished Margaret Lynch had just let Charles Patrick keep that parking space.

Dad attended photography school after his discharge from military service and enjoyed posing for photographs. He was twenty-seven in this 1946 photo. Photo courtesy of Charles and Rutha Patrick's family album.

Dad and Mom were engaged to be married in this 1946 shot taken in Birmingham, Alabama. She was nineteen. Photo courtesy of Charles and Rutha Patrick's family album.

Officer Lynch with wife—Mrs. Margaret Lynch, whose argument over a downtown parking space led to the arrest of Charles Patrick, accompanied her husband to last night's hearing. Officer A. S. Lynch was charged with beating Patrick while he was a City Jail prisoner.

Mr. and Mrs. Lynch are shown arriving for the Jefferson County Civil Service Personnel Board hearing on January 26, 1955. Photo courtesy of *The Birmingham News,* by way of the Department of Archives and Manuscripts, Birmingham Public Library.

Officers Jackson, Siniard with attorney—Officers Earl J. Jackson (left) and J. W. Siniard (right) conferred with their counsel, C. E. Huey, during a recess in their seven-hour hearing before the Personnel Board last night. The two officers were charged with irregularities in connection with the beating of Charles Patrick at the City Jail last month. **NEWS IJAN 2 7 1955'**

Jackson, Huey and Siniard chat during a recess at the Jefferson County Civil Service Personnel Board hearing held January 26, 1955. Photo courtesy of *The Birmingham News,* by way of Birmingham Public Library Department of Archives and Manuscripts.

Dad and Mom were parents of the bride at Christine's 1967 wedding in Los Angeles, California. Photo courtesy of Charles and Rutha Patrick's family album.

Charles and Rutha Patrick in Houston, Texas, celebrating their sixtieth wedding anniversary and attending an event at the Omni Hotel. Photo courtesy of Mignette Y. Patrick Dorsey's family album.

A candid shot of Dad and me in Houston, Texas. Photo courtesy of
Mignette Y. Patrick Dorsey's family album.

Attorney Malcolm L. Wheeler was the powerful lawyer who initially succeeded in getting officers Lynch and Siniard fired, as well as all charges against my father dropped. The officers were later reinstated temporarily. Photo courtesy of M. Wayne Wheeler.

Attorney Peter A. Hall Sr. successfully argued before a panel of three circuit court judges in July 1955 to uphold Officer Lynch's firing from the Birmingham Police Department. Photo courtesy of Peter A. Hall Jr.

Attorney Orzell Billingsley Jr. partnered with Peter A. Hall Sr. in representing Dad before the Jefferson County Civil Service Personnel Board. He was known as the more flamboyant of the two. Photo courtesy of Birmingham Public Library, Department of Archives and Manuscripts.

9
Much Ado 'Bout Civil Rights

A smeared and cleared name, a bruised and healed body, a new baby, a heightened reputation, back to work at ACIPCO—all within sixty days.

Life-altering circumstances can change one's focus. It did not alter Charles Patrick's. My father never wanted to be a hero, only a good husband and father. Inadvertently, he achieved all three. Now it was back to the mundane. Fifteen minutes of fame is a godsend for some. For others, it is a necessary nuisance. But his respite into obscurity would be brief.

Three weeks after the personnel board's ruling, a federal grand jury returned an indictment against Lynch, Siniard and Jackson as a result of the FBI's investigation. The trio appeared before U.S. Commissioner Louise O. Charlton and posted a $300 bond after listening to the counts against them. The federal indictment charged that the three had conspired to deprive Patrick of "rights, privileges and immunities" guaranteed him under the U.S. Constitution. It specifically charged that Lynch did "strike, whip, beat, kick and stomp . . . Charles Patrick," injuring his "chin, lips, chest, back and other parts of his body."[1]

The indictment went on to delineate the five rights of which my father had been deprived from arrest to assault. They included: "1) the right not to be deprived of his liberty without due process of law; 2) the right and privilege to be secure in his person while in the custody of the State of Alabama or an agent or officer thereof; 3) the right and privilege to be immune from summary punishment by persons acting under color of the laws of the State of Alabama; 4) the right and privilege not to be subjected to punishment without due process of law; 5) the right to be tried by due process of law for an alleged offense, and, if found guilty, to be punished in accordance with the laws of the State of Alabama."[2]

Lynch, Siniard and Jackson pleaded not guilty during their formal arraignment before Federal Judge Seybourn H. Lynne. U.S. Attorney Frank M. Johnson Jr. presented the government's case against the officers.

It took four months from the time of the officers' federal indictment to the start of their June 1, 1955, trial. Birmingham attorney Mason Davis was surprised at the short time before the case made it to trial.

Davis, an attorney for nearly half a century, said it could take three years for the circuit court to get a matter from inception to trial and the same was true of federal court. He found it hard to believe that my father "did not have to go back . . . from time to time to testify over the years." But the press had well-documented Lynne's penchant for moving cases quickly off the docket. He was tagged "one of the busiest federal judges in the country . . . [disposing] of an average of three hundred civil and three hundred criminal cases each year."[3]

In the federal case, attorney Roderick Beddow defended Siniard and Jackson while James G. Adams once again represented Lynch. The trial ended even as it began. The proceedings were judged by an "an all-white federal jury" with "few Negroes in the courtroom audience."[4]

Johnson put my father on the witness stand for nearly an hour on June 1, 1955, to relate all the sordid details of the beating. Dad maintained that Lynch was indeed wearing a pistol and a police nightstick during the assault. In a blow to Johnson, Lynne sustained defense objections to Johnson's attempts to show that my father had been acquitted in Recorder's Court of disorderly conduct, the charge for which he was initially arrested.[5]

With Patrick's innocence banned from consideration, the jury was free to focus on the officers' outright lies and insincere drama. It did help that the prosecution was able to show all three defendants were on official duty at the time of the assault, a claim denied in personnel board proceedings. But Siniard's performance on the witness stand added reasonable doubt to the prosecution's case.

On June 2, Siniard was the first defendant to take the stand. Before they went to the Southside jail, he said he cautioned Lynch, "it would not help matters to go to the jail." He then made the following false assertions: that they both left their weapons at the desk before entering the cell block, that Lynch only hit Patrick three or four times with an open palm, that after Patrick fell down he and Jackson picked him up and put him back in his cell, that he and Jackson never touched Patrick "at any time," and that "he did not go to the jail with the intent of beating the prisoner." On cross-examination, Siniard admitted he initially lied about having never gone to the jail.[6]

Lynch testified that he went to the downtown scene where the parking incident happened and found his wife, Margaret, in a highly agitated state. He told the court he went to the jail to question Patrick as to whether he had cursed his wife. He said he struck him "in a fit of rage" after Patrick called his wife a liar.[7]

Beddow's goal was to prove that the entire ordeal was a personal matter between Lynch and Patrick resulting from a verbal exchange involving Margaret Lynch. In his final arguments, Johnson tried to prove that Lynch, Siniard and Jackson "took the law into their own hands, being judge, jury and meting punishment."[8]

It is unclear why news reports included no testimony from any other witnesses. One reporter alluded to the reason: Twenty-five witnesses were "placed under the rule as the trial began and others were on call." Among them was NAACP's Ruby Hurley and other African-Americans with the organization. However, Birmingham attorney Mason Davis explained that just because the testimonies of up to twenty-five witnesses were unpublished does not necessarily mean those witnesses did not testify. Furthermore, federal court records obtained did not include the testimony of the witnesses, only the indictment, Lynne's charge to the jury and various administrative filings.[9]

Lynne, a deacon and men's Bible teacher at Southside Baptist Church, made it impossible for the jury to return a guilty verdict. In his fourteen-page oral charge, the judge noted that while evidence showed the trio was guilty of assault and battery, "that was not what they were on trial for." He instructed the jury "unless you believe beyond a reasonable doubt that Lynch had the purpose in mind of depriving Patrick of his civil rights then he is not guilty under this statute."[10]

Lynne all but sanctioned police brutality in stating that the mere fact that an officer on duty "steps aside from the line and scope of his duties and . . . violate[s] regulations does not mean that they are not acting under the color of their office." The judge must have detected bewilderment stemming from his remarks. He tried to clarify: "What I am trying to say is that not every willful assault by a peace officer amounts to a violation under this [federal] statute." Lynne added that if all Lynch "had in mind was to avenge an insult to himself or his wife . . . he would not be guilty."[11]

Still confusion surfaced at some point during the jury's one-hour deliberation because jury foreman Joe Ezelle asked for clarification of the law. "If we believe that the officers went to the jail deliberately to beat the Negro, are they guilty under the federal charge?"[12]

Considering the initial federal indictment, the answer would seem obvious. Three of the rights in question were: "the right to be secure in his person while in custody of the law, the right to be immune from summary punishment by persons acting under color of the laws of . . .

Alabama, and the right not to be subjected to punishment without due process."[13]

Yet such matters are subject to interpretation, and Lynne narrowed the issue down to whether the officers went to the jail specifically intending to "deprive the Negro of his right to trial."[14]

Never mind the other rights of which Patrick might have been deprived. And so the federal circus ended. The all-white jury before a mostly white audience acquitted Lynch, Siniard and Jackson. The guilty walked as Margaret Lynch sat in the back of the courtroom . . . and sobbed.[15]

Charles Patrick had spoken truth to power, but at the federal level, the latter prevailed.

Lynne was known as a staunch upholder of laws hostile to African-Americans. A black couple arrested and charged with disorderly conduct for occupying a white waiting room at the Birmingham train station sued in 1957. Recorder's Court dropped the charges; Lynne tossed out the lawsuit. Another suit filed by a black barber in November 1960 sat on Lynne's docket until October 1962. Such experiences with the feds convinced blacks that "the behavior of Judge Lynne . . . was exposing the truth that the federal judiciary was unlikely to hand blacks their rights without a struggle."[16]

On the other hand, history holds a different view of Johnson, who six months after the Patrick case was appointed a U.S. district court judge—serving alongside Lynne. Johnson was most famous for the 1956 ruling that led to the desegregation of Montgomery, Alabama's, buses and parks, a case that followed Rosa Parks's arrest for refusing to give up her bus seat to a white passenger. On the three-judge panel, Lynne was the dissenting vote.[17]

Despite Lynne's handling of the Patrick case, it was nonetheless remarkable that the FBI took the time to investigate, submit its findings and secure a federal indictment. However, James A. Robey Sr. might have paid with his career for his effectiveness in investigating the officers.

Robey Jr. said his father had received superior evaluations under J. Edgar Hoover up until the time of the Patrick case. But after the federal indictment of Lynch, Siniard and Jackson, his father was given a bad performance review and ordered to relocate to New Orleans, a move Robey Sr. considered a demotion. So rather than be demoted, he retired from the FBI in the fall of 1955. Ironically, in February and March of 1956, Robey Sr.'s replacement, Special Agent-in-Charge D. W. Fults, held a series of lectures on the topic of civil rights violations. His audience? Birmingham police officers.[18]

The FBI's skillful handling of the investigation was matched by the methodic, detailed reporting by reporters Alice Gardner Murphy of the *Birmingham News* and Edward Pilley and Don Cummins of the *Post-Herald.*

Their stories were far more detailed than case action summaries. They read like legal records. Indeed, Murphy had the foresight to seek out Solicitor Emmett Perry and ask if under federal law the trio could be charged with assault and battery. Perry told her it would be unlawful because "such charges would have to be instituted by the city police department or the injured party."[19]

The *Birmingham World*'s front-page news coverage of my father's case was expected since it was black-owned. Yet white-owned press coverage was not only constant, but fair. An exception was Cummins' regular use of the word "alleged" when describing the beating. Pilley and Murphy wrote as though the jail beating happened without a doubt.[20]

The *Birmingham News* and *Post-Herald* newspapers had received criticism on two fronts. The Northern press accused the white-owned publications of unfair coverage of its African-American citizens. On the other hand, Birmingham's police officers criticized them for the "playing up of cases of alleged brutality, without disclosure of the policeman's side." So resentful were some in the city that Klansmen once burned a cross in front of the Mountain Brook home of *News* publisher Clarence Hanson.[21]

Howell Raines observed, "It was not a common occurrence, but the *News* and *Post-Herald* gave prominent coverage to some racial cases." Some of it he called courageous, specifically the reporting that followed the Dynamite Hill bombings where black citizens—such as the family of political and civil rights activist Angela Davis—who had moved into areas previously zoned for whites endured constant bombings of their homes.[22]

By the summer of 1955, my father had achieved what he had wanted most—exoneration. The federal fiasco ended in victory for the defendants, and Dad was left with freedom intact.

Arthur and Margaret Lynch might have celebrated in whatever way such couples did at that time. Yet the fête surely ended nearly thirty days later when attorney Peter A. Hall Sr. argued before a panel of three circuit court judges to uphold Lynch's firing from the Birmingham Police Department.

Perhaps the *Birmingham World*'s front-page newspaper headline said it best: "3-Judge Panel Upholds Firing of Policeman."[23]

Truth to Power— A Movement Missed

Citizens rant about putting an end to police brutality. True. The latter cannot be tolerated. Yet like Frodo Baggins's ring in *The Lord of the Rings,* the curse of power is the temptation to abuse it.

Some police officers cannot resist that temptation. But that is true of any human who possesses power, however fleeting. Many will at one time or another act in a way to abuse it. Watch two children at play. The one who is taller and older will usually eventually bully the shorter, younger one—probably sooner than later. The temptation is just too great. In that context, steady episodes of police brutality are not surprising.

Officers Lynch, Siniard and Jackson were part of a Southern society that continued to abuse its power long after slavery ended. Yet if there is a positive aspect to the wretched tendency to abuse power, it is that such abuse sometimes elicits unusual courage from its victims. Such was the case with Charles Patrick.

There is a force greater than abusive power: truth. When Patrick spoke truth to power from December 1954 to June 1955, he became a fulcrum, a point of convergence for two races. Although Birmingham's white and black populations were segregated, many whites joined blacks in singing the same song, one that demanded justice for Patrick. And conflict erupted.

Truth to power pit one policeman against another, police chief against commissioner, commissioner against mayor, white citizen against white citizen, press against political powers. It fueled debate: *"What is wrong with hiring black police officers?"* It left Birmingham reeling, white people standing next to black, both wondering, *"What just happened?"*

Truth to power caused motives to collide. Politicians saw a chance to curry favor with constituents. White citizens hopped on the opportunity to change Northern views of Southerners by firing off letters to the press in support of a black man. The white press used the occasion to improve its poor record of reporting on black citizens. Blacks saw a springboard, a platform to demand the hiring of black policemen. The beating had something in it for everyone, except Charles Patrick, who just wanted to clear his name, go to Los Angeles, California, and raise his family.

Perhaps the entire ordeal with Margaret Lynch happened because of my father's mindset. He did not view the woman the way she viewed herself.

To Dad, Mrs. Lynch was a mere human being who took a parking space for which he had been waiting. To Mrs. Lynch, Dad was a mere black man, which meant she was entitled to the parking space for which he had been waiting. Dad's objections stemmed from his beliefs; Mrs. Lynch's insolence stemmed from hers. It is doubtful Mrs. Lynch would have demanded the parking space had Charles Patrick been a white man or white woman, even with her husband being a police officer.

Racial superiority is aroused when confronted by the race over which it feels superior. The parking space was her right, her privilege, however unearned. The belief led to actions that hurt another person. "The problem is the depravity of white, the unjust exercise of power in a white-supremacist society, the unearned privileges that come with whiteness," explained Dr. Robert Jensen, professor of journalism at the University of Texas-Austin.[1]

Under Jim Crow thinking, prejudiced whites held demeaning expectations of blacks, which meant blacks were expected to treat whites with reverence. Failure to observe this code could result in physical assaults, even death.[2]

My father discovered that. Margaret Lynch was incensed because Dad violated the code. After all, she got her parking space. Officer Lynch was inflamed, not so much because his wife had to bicker for a parking space, but because a black man had violated the code.

Black reporter and historian Geraldine H. Moore once wrote that Birmingham "before the sixties was a city in which two separate and distinct communities existed, and to a large extent, were hostile to each other."[3]

The beating, public outcry, Patrick acquittal and subsequent punishment of officers Lynch and Siniard did not remedy the problem Moore described. Rather, the Patrick episode simply produced a common point around which both races rallied—for a brief period. Yet for once, Birmingham became sick of itself, and coughed up justice.

Birmingham's white citizens in 1954 did what Jensen believes is incumbent upon any white person when unearned privileges come at the expense of others: "reject the system that conditions your pleasure on someone else's pain."[4]

Yet, perhaps the saddest thing concerning Birmingham was that after ridding itself of segregationist police commissioner Eugene "Bull" Connor, the epitome of power corrupted, the citizenry returned him to power, setting the bloody stage on which Reverend Fred Shuttlesworth, Dr. Martin Luther King Jr., Ralph Abernathy, Arthur Shores, Peter A. Hall Sr., Orzell Billingsley Jr. and countless others, bravely fought.[5]

Nevertheless, my father believed things got better for Birmingham's blacks after his ordeal. I had a hard time accepting that. In fact, it appeared things got worse, especially after Connor returned to power in 1957. It was as though the man was on a mission to humble a people who had forgotten their place during his four-year hiatus. One wonders if he fancied . . . *Black folk running around accusing police officers, demanding we hire black cops, even our good white citizens getting out of place, writ-*

ing letters denouncing our white power base—and all because my boys beat a Negro? Yes. Connor had a lot of work to do.

It is believed Connor, Birmingham's bad boy, did much to advance civil rights.[6] Troubling though the converse logic may be, it is true. Police Commissioner Connor was one of the primary antagonists who unwittingly helped launch the Birmingham civil rights movement just by being himself. He aroused the ire and defiance of a people tired of being oppressed. And as a result, the civil rights story unfolded.

Connor, however, was self-destructive. His adulterous affair in the early 1950s was one of the reasons he did not seek reelection as police commissioner in 1953. But if the indiscretion indirectly led to his ouster, supremacist reaction to the momentum African-American activists and white progressives gained from the Charles Patrick brutality case may have helped ferry Connor back to power in 1957.

There had been numerous calls for the Birmingham Police Department to hire African-American patrolmen for areas of the city where black residents lived.

A 1952 citizen report on the police department recommended that the city commission "make a careful study of the desirability of employment of a limited number of Negro officers—say eight—and their assignment to duties involving only the Negro population." The authors were careful to clarify that they were not "recommending the immediate employment of Negro police," only an "unprejudiced study."[7]

Connor opposed any such hiring, once telling the Junior Chamber of Commerce, "As long as I am police commissioner . . . I will never put them on here." To their credit, the authors of the citizen report had previously said of Connor: "He is deficient in executive ability and lacks an objective outlook."[8] Perhaps another reason Connor wisely chose not to seek reelection to his post in 1953.

However, the one factor Connor had on his side was Birmingham's culture. White supremacists had proven to be as powerful as any other group when united behind a common agenda. Fortunately, the 1954 Patrick beating occurred during Connor's absence, thus the favorable outcome. More important, the case also reintroduced the call for the hiring of African-American police officers.

Historian Andrew M. Manis punctuated this in Reverend Fred L. Shuttlesworth's biography, noting, "During the first half of 1955, the Patrick incident sparked more frequent and insistent calls for the hiring of African-Americans by the police department."[9]

At its January 16, 1955, mass meeting, the NAACP not only drafted a resolution deploring the reinstatement of the officers who assaulted my father, but they also used the incident to herald the hiring of black police officers.[10]

The black policeman controversy had a two-pronged effect: It aroused Connor, the supremacist, and Shuttlesworth, the activist, "eventually bringing Shuttlesworth to center stage and contributing to the return of Connor to power in 1957."[11]

In February 1955, Pattie came out in support of the city hiring female officers, but stopped short of endorsing black males. Then after Reverend George Rudolph made a June 21, 1955, appeal for the city to hire black officers, Mayor Morgan publicly came out in favor of the idea, a plan commissioners Lindbergh and Bradley opposed. Morgan told the commission, "I have discussed the situation with officials of her [Alabama's] Southern cities. I haven't [had] one official say that Negro policemen haven't been entirely satisfactory."[12]

Just what the reverend needed. Shuttlesworth wasted no time. He drafted a petition calling for the hiring of black officers and circulated it among the city's ministers, succeeding in getting seventy-seven to sign it. Then he presented it to the city commission on Monday, July 25—a month after Rudolph had appeared before the same body. The commission was sympathetic but hesitant, ever mindful of the powerful voting block of the city's "lower-status white electorate" that would eventually return Connor to power. Undeterred, Shuttlesworth collected 4,500 signatures from black residents and 119 from white. In addition, the Young Men's Business Club sent an August 1, 1955, letter to the city commission asking that "arrangements be made whereby examinations for policemen be opened to Negroes."[13]

Unfortunately, the August 28, 1955, murder of Emmett Till in Mississippi hurt Shuttlesworth's September 1 appearance before the Birmingham City Commission. With racial tension awash nationwide, Mayor Morgan chilled, tabling Shuttlesworth's request and prompting the latter to declare, "Emmett Till's death had nothing to do with Negro police. You are telling us that you won't give them to us; we'll have to fight to get them."[14]

The NAACP elected Shuttlesworth membership chairman, but a May 1956 court injunction outlawed the NAACP's executive board, effectively barring it from operating in Alabama. This spurred him to join with other ministers to form the Alabama Christian Movement for Human Rights (ACMHR) in June 1956.

However, not all blacks endorsed the new organization, including Orzell Billingsley Jr. and Reverend M. W. Whitt, Charles Patrick's attorney and pastor respectively.

This split between "the elite Negro classes" and the "black masses" marked the emergence of more aggressive black activist groups that "demanded immediate and equal access to the system." Dr. Martin Luther King Jr. would refer to them as "New Negroes," who appealed to a mass base and eventually joined forces with national movement groups. Historian Eskew wrote: "The interplay of these forces combined with the resistance of Southern white people marked the emergence of the civil rights movement."[15]

The movement in Birmingham got its Southern white resistance from Connor, who defeated Lindbergh in a 1957 runoff. Connor actually ran on his record as a staunch racist segregationist, slamming Lindbergh for being too soft on segregation. With the "white lower middle class" catapulting him to victory by a margin of 103 votes, the face-off between

Shuttlesworth and Connor was on. As Eskew noted, "Lindbergh's inability to win reelection underscored Birmingham's failure to carry out the positive race reforms he had proposed during his four-year term. With Bull Connor back in office, Birmingham prepared for a showdown with the civil rights movement."[16]

National civil rights groups were already in league with Birmingham thanks to Shuttlesworth's leadership and the ACMHR. But Connor's "made-to-order legal violence" heightened suffering under the city's white power structure and required a different kind of force.[17]

Shuttlesworth battled Connor in Birmingham from 1957 on into the 1960s. But he needed help. As he told Howell Raines: "It gradually [came] into my mind the idea that we needed some different type of confrontation . . . Here I thought, with 'Bull' Connor being the epitome of segregation and SCLC [Southern Christian Leadership Conference] being organized by us to change it, the two forces should be met . . . so it was at my invitation, my personal invitation . . . that Dr. King and Ralph Abernathy and the SCLC boys agreed to come in."[18]

The result was that the national struggle for civil rights reached its climax in the city of Birmingham. Connor's water hoses and police dog blunders in the spring of 1963, the arrest of King and other prominent civil rights leaders, the murder of children in the bombing of the Sixteenth Street Baptist Church—all placed the city in national focus. These events provided embarrassing media footage that captured the attention of President John F. Kennedy and led to the passage of the Civil Rights Act of 1964.[19]

People worldwide generally have come to associate the name Dr. Martin Luther King Jr. with America's national movement against racial oppression. Raines said King's letter written from the Birmingham jail "established King once and for all as the spokesman for the movement and for black America." But that did not bother Shuttlesworth, who though he continued his involvement in Birmingham, eventually moved to Cincinnati, Ohio, to pastor a flock. Yet he initially believed King's letter should have been jointly signed by SCLC leaders, "simply because we had agreed to do things together, you know . . . but I guess as I look at it now . . . I think King deserves all the credit . . . He was the spokesman, and he was the one that God had chose to be the charismatic person for that age."[20]

I asked my father if he had met Dr. King, and if the civil rights leader knew about his case. My father said he may have known, "but he never got in contact with me because he was on one side and I was trying to save myself on the other side."

The irony is that both men mingled with the same black power brokers in Birmingham prior to the start of mass, organized resistance to oppression. And news reports would put them within days of each other at different NAACP events. Historical contemporaries, the two men kept missing each other.

I called Shuttlesworth on April 20, 2006. Having read much about him, having stared at his statue outside the Birmingham Civil Rights Institute, having photographed my father standing next to it, I desperately wanted to interview the man. If nothing else but to thank him for running with the black policeman issue, a platform popularized by Dad's case.

"Reverend Shuttlesworth, do you remember the Charles Patrick case?" I eagerly asked him. He paused and humbly answered that he did not, adding there had been so much he had gone through since 1954.

It was okay. I smiled and thanked him. He had invited me to call him back the next day. I did not.

Shuttlesworth is like a fearless general who has fought more battles than most. Yet it was hard to accept that even the memories of generals fade. Fortunately, documented historical facts do not.

Charles Patrick's story is part of the civil rights story. His courageous actions laid a foundation for the movement, and dramatized for the oppressed African-Americans of Birmingham in 1954 that fortitude and truth in the face of power can prevail.

I asked my father if he believed the whole Birmingham civil rights movement might have begun over a dispute about a parking space. He stopped short of making that bold claim, but said after his acquittal and after the officers' dismissal from the force, "They [the police] stopped coming to your house and beating you up." He said, "Things started getting better."

Then he added something that surprised me, considering all he had championed.

"Well, actually it happened when the lady wouldn't give up her seat in Montgomery—after those things happened to me."

Of course, he referred to Rosa Parks. It was then that I discovered Parks was his hero. I also realized he was clueless as to the pivotal role he had played in precipitating the civil rights movement in Birmingham.

What Dad did not understand was that Parks had attended training sessions at Highlander Center in Tennessee, a facility dedicated to "participatory democracy" whereby the socially conscious of different races gathered to strategize solutions to the social ills in their respective communities. At Highlander, Parks learned how to conduct herself if arrested, and like all participants, she was challenged upon leaving to return home and take action, do something about whatever pressing societal problem stirred her. In addition, if former attendees needed administrative support to carry out their charge, Highlander staff provided it.[21]

For fun, I once asked my father what he thought about Highlander.

"Highlander club for *what?*" he asked.

The Highlander experience was not Charles Patrick's experience. He had no training in the etiquette of proper passive resistance. Dad had only a high school education, military training and some photography training. But what he lacked in education, he made up for in raw courage and moral values instilled by parents, teachers, clergy, the military and the black community.

What Parks and Patrick shared, however, was courage in the face of sudden injustice, followed by refusal to ride easy fame handed to them.

"No one had planned for *me* to get arrested, including myself," Parks once said. She was simply too tired to stand in response to the bus driver's orders. Furthermore, she said, "I didn't feel that I was breaking any law."[22]

Likewise, my father decidedly, naturally, confronted Mrs. Lynch over her taking a parking space for which he had been waiting. He did not think his protest was breaking any law. It was as natural a reaction as snatching a child about to step off a curb into traffic, even as natural as pursuing Mrs. Lynch's husband and his accomplices after they beat him.

Parks chose to take a less active role in the Montgomery bus boycott that followed her arrest. [23] Patrick, too, settled back into the mundane, the routine, eagerly.

What pains me is that my father could have chosen to play a sustained, active and leading role in one of the most unique and historic organized mass movements in the history of the struggle against racial oppression in the United States. But he chose to miss it.

After my father's courageous stand, African-American defiance before abusive powers emerged as the norm in Birmingham. The city did change, ultimately.

Shuttlesworth was right. "But for Birmingham, we would not be here today."[24]

Yet before any movement where people march en masse for basic civil rights denied, there are fuzzy accounts of individual courage, the details of which are often buried safely within the memories of the participants themselves.

Thanks, Dad, for sharing those memories.

Epilogue

The Cure for the Southern Headache

Not much made Charles Patrick run. He was fully aware that some wanted to kill him over what happened to Lynch, Siniard and Jackson. Nonetheless, living in Birmingham did not faze him.

"I know I would be in heaven with God," he said. "That's where I'm looking to go when I do leave this world."

But there was something of which he was afraid. Something that did make him run, far away. It happened in July 1955, after Lynch lost his appeal to regain his job, and as Shuttlesworth scurried here and there building a case for the hiring of black policemen.

My stepbrother, Carl, was a newspaper delivery boy. On a July 1955 afternoon, as he was throwing newspapers, four or five white men appeared next to him in a car. My father recalled the day, speaking hesitantly, reliving it.

"Hey boy," they yelled. "Ain't Charles Patrick your daddy?"

My brother said, "Yes, sir."

"And this is your route right here?"

"Yes, sir," my brother replied.

"Thank you," they said, and drove away.

Fifty-plus years later, he could still recall what they said to his son. "That was a threat. I had to get away from there to save my family," he explained. Dad tried as best he could to prepare everyone. "I told them

Daddy had to leave this place and [they had to] go with me and Rutha and Marydeane," he said.

Again, the churches—with Harmony Street's Reverend Whitt leading the charge—pulled together and offered financial assistance. "Go ahead, get out of this place," Dad said many advised. "And they still kept helping me until we left and went to California."

I recall a prayer, one my father said he prayed from the time he married my mother in 1946. It might have gone something like this: *Lord, let me go to Los Angeles, California, to become a postman.* Amen.

My mother never did want to go to Los Angeles. She constantly badgered Dad about staying in Birmingham. Had she relented earlier, the argument with Margaret Lynch over that parking space might never have happened. Mom had learned her lesson.

"Well, I was concerned about his safety so I didn't bother anymore about Charles wanting to go," she said. "But I wasn't going. I was going to stay home and let him see if he could find a job out there, then send for us."

A talk with one of her teachers was enough to change her mind, a talk that sparked memories of a certain wisdom.

Her grandmother had once warned years prior to never let her husband go to work in another city without her.

"Because once he's in another city, it's just a natural thing that will happen. When you get back together, he will have been someone else's husband, too," Mom said Grandma Virgin had advised. My mother didn't want that. "So I said, 'Let me get on up and get out of here.'"

My parents sold or gave away their furniture, packed clothes and linens and left, taking the children to various relatives. Rutha Jr. and Gregg went to live with our great-uncle Bud; and Carl, Charles Jr. and Larry were taken to our great-grandmother, Grandma Virgin, a godly and beautiful woman of African, Italian and Native American descent. My parents took seven-month-old Marydeane to California with them.

When Dad and Mom left Birmingham in a two-door Ford in July of

1955, they had no idea how far California was. They thought they could arrive in one day. Reality surfaced and they soon pulled over on the shoulder of Route 66.

"A highway patrolman came by and saw us and just let us sleep," he said. "The next day I woke up and went to Tucumcari where I spent [the] night . . . That was the only place you could stay on the way."

I knew the route. So does anyone familiar with Nat King Cole's "Route 66." What the singer did not elaborate on in his famous hit, however, was the fact that people who looked like him could not rent a motel room or eat in a restaurant along that route if a white person owned it.

Traveling African-Americans in the 1950s knew the spots that offered respite, and they would drive long hours without sleep to get there. It was primarily the Latino-owned motels that were friendly to blacks traveling Route 66. My father knew of those in Tucumcari, New Mexico.

New Mexico was my father's first encounter with the kindness of Latino citizens. I hated that he used the word "Mexicans," but that was acceptable back then, just as today one would not say "Negro" or "Colored"—unless you are Charles Patrick.

As for restaurants, packing long-lasting snacks in an ice chest guaranteed a meal. The staples were fried chicken, Spam, Vienna sausages, tuna, crackers, cheese and Kool-Aid. My parents spread out a blanket and ate at rest stops along Route 66. And relieving themselves at a gasoline station was out of the question. My parents would open the car doors and crouch behind them for privacy.

"You couldn't use restrooms in the Southern states at the time," my father said. "You'd go in the back of the place [filling station] and they had a hole in the ground . . . like an outhouse and spiders and everything was in that hole."

My father had notified Johnny Dudley and Buddy Pope of his pending arrival in Los Angeles. "They had a job there for him," Mom said. "So he went to work at the end of the week."

Dad's friends spoke to a foreman at Layne & Bowler Pump Company, a foundry in East Los Angeles. Like that, he was hired. My mother was also fortunate. Arriving on a Sunday evening, she went job hunting Monday morning.

"Had [driven] 2,200 and something miles and went to work the next day," she laughed. "But I guess that's youth."

She started work at a garment factory downtown and stayed for about two pay periods, then left for an alterations job at Gary's Tuxedo Shop.

In Los Angeles, they lived with Maxibell and Buddy Pope on the second floor of a two-story house located near Vernon Avenue. The Popes did not charge them rent. "We just bought our own food," Mom said.

Maxibell kept the baby, Marydeane, while they worked. Plans were to save up money for about two months, then return to Alabama for the other five children, but by August 1955, my father encountered an unbelievable opportunity.

"I didn't have any money. The job was giving everyone a check for two weeks vacation," he said. "I went in the office and told the man . . . 'I wish you would consider me so that I can go and get my children.'" Though on the job for less than a month, the manager surprisingly gave him a two-week vacation because he was a good worker.

"And I knew then that God was in the plan," Dad said.

Four friends left California with Dad to help with driving and expenses. The two Hispanic men he dropped off in Albuquerque, New Mexico; the two black men he ferried to Birmingham. Mom stayed behind in Los Angeles and worked.

But the journey was trouble-filled.

"I had two flats and I had to get a new tire," he said. "On the highway, we got Mexican tire places, and they'd go in and find a tire to put on and then they would balance them."

Gathering the five children from various Alabama counties was easy, but before leaving, he ran into more trouble. The Ford's transmission belts needed tightening. My father said a white mechanic in Birmingham did the work.

"The gentleman fixed my car up and didn't charge me a penny," Dad said, proudly. "He gassed my car up and I paid him for the gas, and they didn't say anything."

The journey back to Los Angeles involved traveling many hours through California's Mojave Desert. Towns like Needles and Barstow were unbearable, even at night. His fortune being what it was, he was forced to stop in a desert town to sleep on the shoulder. He drifted off— and awoke to protest.

"My children said, 'Daddy, it's too hot here. Let's go!' And the Lord was with me. I opened my eyes and drove that car and got back home in front of Buddy and Maxibell Pope's house and that steering wheel wouldn't turn to the left or the right."

The steering column had completely rusted.

"God brought me back there," my father said.

The Patrick family prospered in Los Angeles. Ramona, named after his great-grandmother, Princess Mona, was born a year later. My father left the foundry to drive milk trucks for Golden State Dairy. Eventually, they bought a house on W. 86th Place off Broadway near Manchester.

Then one day in 1957, Charles Patrick walked into the U.S. Post Office, filled out a job application and was hired as a letter carrier without having to take the test.

"He was a veteran," my mother said. "They were partial to veterans."

Dad had another explanation. "I knew I could be a postman in California . . . and the Lord fulfilled my dreams."

Then trouble ensued. Carl, whose nickname was Spooky, got involved in a gang and a judge ordered him back to Chicago to live with his mother. Dad said he gave Carl a suit and a pair of Stacy Adams shoes and bid him adieu in 1959. Carl did return in 1971, but he and Dad did not mesh. He died on July 12, 1995, the second of my siblings to depart. The first to die was Rutha Jr.

Mom met a woman who was leaving Los Angeles due to a heart condition. When my mother told her about Rutha's rheumatic fever, the woman was horrified. "Oh, don't bring her here!" she said. "I give her about five years and she'll be dead."

That was on August 18, 1955. My sister, Rutha Patrick Jr., died August 18, 1960, at the age of thirteen, but not from rheumatic fever. During a hospital stay, medical staff accidentally administered the wrong medicine to Rutha. It killed her.

Fortunately for my parents, they had another newborn to distract them from their grief. I was two months old when Rutha died. My mother said every time she fell into depression after the death, I would wake up and scream nonstop. This happened constantly, and having to tend to my needs helped keep Mom out of the doldrums. Because of that, I was called the miracle baby.

In 1963, our family of eight relocated to a much larger house on Denker Avenue in South Central Los Angeles. A Spanish style with tile roof, it had a massive room attached to the garage where the boys lived. They threw wild weekend parties back there. My father would sit on the front porch holding a shotgun, charging twenty-five cents a head. My brothers gave Dad a small cut from the proceeds and they kept the rest. Parties ended when Dad told the teens to leave, usually around 2 a.m. If they ignored the verbal order, he would fire the weapon in the air, instantly dispersing the crowd.

My father made many trips to and from Mexico during the 1960s. Before each trip, he would order us to rid our closets of clothing and shoes we had outgrown as well as toys we did not need.

I understood after becoming an adult why Dad drove us across the border to Mexicali, Mexico, to deliver food and other items to poor families. I believe it was his way of expressing gratitude for the kindnesses Hispanic citizens extended to him along Route 66.

On one occasion, a young boy, Pedro, took a liking to our family. Pedro, who was about four, would run alongside our station wagon until it disappeared down a dusty Mexico road. He was one of what seemed like a dozen or more children in his family.

One day my father asked me, "Do you want a little brother?" I loved Pedro because we played together, and I was not much bigger than he was.

Like choosing a toy, I told my father I wanted him. Dad got the attention of his mother, pointed to Pedro and then to our car. I remember her shaking her head vigorously. Then she snatched Pedro and held him close. I took it I would not be getting a little brother. I sometimes think about Pedro. We never saw the family again.

Christine arrived from Birmingham and lived with us for a short time in the early 1960s. She later married and earned a Ph.D.

My father was once asked how Los Angeles differed from Birmingham. He said it was not segregated, and they could all attend the same church. Speaking of which, one Sunday my parents visited Freewill Missionary Baptist Church. My mother had had a dream years prior about the inside of a church. When she walked into Freewill, it was a replica of the one in her dream. They joined.

At Freewill, Dad rose up through the religious ranks, soon becoming chairman of the trustee board. He was the formidable Deacon Patrick, who whipped his three sons with a razor strap he got from a barber (other fathers often borrowed it) and pampered his girls like dolls.

The guys at the church loved him because he ran the church's Teen Post, a government-funded program for inner-city youth. Fishing, camping, hunting trips, fish fries, barbecues, weekend parties, sleepovers in the big back room—Dad showered the teenaged boys with attention and good times. Most important, he kept them off the streets. That, too, ended. Funding for inner-city programs like that was eliminated. The teenaged boys had nowhere to go. Consequently, the early 1970s saw the rise of gangs; some attributed this to teenage ennui.

One of the toughest periods for my parents raising six children in South Central Los Angeles was the August 1965 Watts Riots. "Burn, baby, burn," the slogan disc jockey Magnificent Montague made famous, was not permitted in the Patrick home, nor was the raised, clenched fist, signifying black power.

Dad was too military, too patriotic for such nonsense. Of course, we screamed "Burn, baby, burn!" and tossed that clenched fist as high as we could when he was not around. I was only five, but my siblings did it, so I did, too.

The riots were followed by the rise of the Black Power Movement, Black Panthers, Angela Davis, Motown, black action movies, dashikis, Afros, bell-bottom pants, the Beatles, Jimi Hendrix, hippies, nudist camps, free love and sex, too, LSD, marijuana, and more. Even the earthquakes were original.

I remember the 1968 Olympics when the track-and-field guys raised clenched fists instead of solemnly covering their hearts during the national anthem. My father ranted in disgust for months. His children?

"*Ungawa*! Black power! *Ungawa*! Black Power!"[1]

It was baffling. America had treated him so badly after World War II. Yet here he was demanding his children respect the flag. He considered rebellion and radicalism in the absence of the type of oppression he had endured in Birmingham unpatriotic rabble-rousing. I suppose he thought: *You've never had to drink from a Colored water fountain!*

The Watts Riots happened just days after President Lyndon Johnson signed the Voting Rights Act into law and only months after the nation witnessed the events of Bloody Sunday in Selma, Alabama. Images of white officers beating black protestors were seen by all, including angry Southern California African-Americans.[2]

Dignity deflated by unemployment, dilapidated schools, blighted housing conditions, blacks in Watts were mad, real mad. Yet the reverse television images of blacks beating whites during the riots had as much of an effect on white America as did the opposite on blacks nation-wide.

According to historian Robert J. Norrell, "Watts instantaneously altered the image that African-Americans projected into the national media—from the long-suffering and peaceful southern Negro to the thieving, fire-bombing black racists of urban Los Angeles."[3]

Norrell argued that after Watts, whites felt threatened.

"Watts canceled the expectation among sympathetic whites, and many African-Americans, too, that the great reforms of 1964 and 1965 would bring forth a time of racial harmony."[4]

Whites recoiled with white flight. They fled to the hills and oceanside communities as more blacks crowded into South Central Los Angeles. They scurried to the valleys, the canyons. Whites went as far west, south, north and east as they could to get away from their black neighbors.

The violent militancy of African-Americans in Los Angeles affected my father as well. The rioting and pillaging was alarming. Dad wanted peace, assimilation into society, integrated neighborhoods, schools and churches.

Dad had witnessed progress in Birmingham. Memories of white citizens writing letters on his behalf inspired hope. It was ironic that he shared more of the same values with progressive white Southerners than he did with rioting blacks in Watts. Furthermore, he did not like the militancy he saw brewing in his own children.

Los Angeles, the city he thought would erase his Southern headache, had substituted a migraine. I think Dad wanted to run, too, back to Southern comfort.

It was around this time I remember him threatening to move the family back to Birmingham. Those threats produced severe anxiety attacks, like the ones that came on whenever my mother mused aloud that I needed braces.

Never having encountered the hate-inspired white terrorism my parents did desensitized me to black oppression. Though I read the articles about my father, I could not put his ordeal, his unprecedented heroism, into perspective. The South was anathema. Los Angeles cured for me whatever headache it gave my parents.

But inevitably, the rebellion and militancy of the 1960s and 1970s left us. In the midst of social turmoil, my parents had reared us exactly the way they were reared. And we returned to that strict upbringing. Larry enlisted in the military. The rest of us settled down. Some ended up born-again Christians, knocking on doors, telling folk about Jesus, shaking their heads in disgust at those wild teenagers with no respect for authority. By the mid 1970s, the only children left at home were Gregg, Ramona and me.

Dad frequently permitted people in need of a home to live with us— unknown vagrants sometimes who shared the large garage bedroom with Gregg, but something he did one year shocked us.

Larry had befriended a European youth while stationed in Greece. I remember the call. He pleaded with Dad to sponsor the young man in the United States—and allow him to live with the family. My mother protested. He was a high school senior and she had two teenage daughters at home. No way. But Dad prevailed, arguing that God might have a plan for the teen and he wanted to be a part of whatever his future might hold. With my brother sending money to help offset expenses, we welcomed a white European with a thick accent into our home.

Upon his arrival, Dad immediately took him shopping for a more American-looking wardrobe, and allowed him to live in the garage bedroom with Gregg. He was enrolled in a school farther away where the student body was primarily white. One time, the young man was confronted by thugs who stole the leather coat Larry had given him. From that day on, my mother chauffeured him to and from school to protect him from newly formed inner-city gangs.

My parents spoke lovingly of him in his absence, and my father ordered the entire family to treat the teen as a brother. And we did, even warning hoodlums that the Greek youth in the neighborhood was ours. There were other family sacrifices too numerous to list. The young man soon graduated, married and eventually returned to Europe.

My parents cradled a white youth in their home. No sermon on racial unity ever said as much to me.

Mom and Dad eventually made good on their threats to return to Birmingham, Alabama. It happened years after I graduated from high school. An ill-timed, mild stroke ended my father's beloved career as a postman, intensifying his longing for Birmingham. So with their children grown, they sold the house on Denker Avenue, packed up and moved back home in 1984.

At first they lived with my grandfather in Eastlake before building their dream home nearby. Dad was pleased to see that Birmingham had changed during the decades he was away. He said it was "a lot different" and boasted that the city had a "colored mayor."

He added that he did not feel afraid anymore because he knew God was with him. He now found the past amusing. "We had 'White supremacy for the right. Thank God for white supremacy!'" He laughed, then a moment of serious reflection: "We went through burning hell. See how things change? Just like the wind blows the tumbleweed, the bottom comes up on the top. Now we love each other."

A white man kicked my father's chin open when he was thirty-six years old. At ninety-one, there is a deep, vertical indentation where smooth skin used to be.

"The only scar I ever had on my body," Dad lamented. "I can shave around it."

Afterword

There is regret. It involves the piano my parents either gave away or sold.

After relocating to California, my father heard rumors that fired police officer Arthur S. Lynch took a job with a furniture moving company—and that a piano fell on him.

I regret that I can only wonder.

Notes

Preface

1. Jerome A. Cooper, December 30, 1954, James W. Morgan Mayoral Papers, File #266.21.23. Department of Archives and Manuscripts, Birmingham Public Library (hereafter BPLA),

Chapter 1

1. Glenn T. Eskew, *But for Birmingham* (Chapel Hill and London: The University of North Carolina Press, 1997), 53–54.

2. Reverend Garry B. Slaughter, "Church History Summary" (program for Harmony Street Baptist Church 117th Homecoming Celebration), November 6, 2005.

Chapter 2

1. Eskew, *But for Birmingham*, 96.

2. Ibid., 94–95.

3. "Police Accused of Beating Man," *Birmingham Post-Herald*, December 31, 1954.

4. Eskew, *But for Birmingham*, 95.

5. "Two Policemen Fired in Beating of Prisoner," *Birmingham News*, December 21, 1954; "Two Policemen Fired on Charge of Beating Negro," *Birmingham Post-Herald*, December 21, 1954, and January 27, 1955; "Jail-cell Beating Police Before City Commissioners," *Birmingham World*, December 28, 1954.

6. "Personnel Board Hearing—Two Witnesses Tell of City Jail Beating," *Birmingham News*, January 27, 1955.

7. William Morgan, *Illustrations of Masonry, By One of the Fraternity Who Has Devoted Thirty Years to the Subject* (Cincinnati, Ohio: Matthew Gardner, 1850), 80.

8. "Chief Orders Investigation into Charge that Officer Beat Prisoner," *Birmingham Post-Herald*, December 18, 1954; "Probe Ordered—Man Testifies in Court that Officer Beat Him," *Birmingham News*, December 18, 1954.

Chapter 3

1. James Tarlton, "Birmingham Jail," 1923, Birmingham Public Library.

2. Charles Morgan, Jr., *A Time to Speak* (New York: Harper & Row, 1964), 42.

3. Information about Malcolm L. Wheeler was provided by a close associate of Wheeler's during telephone conversations with the author on July 9, 2007, and September 8, 2009. In that the interview was conducted in confidentiality, the name has been withheld by mutual agreement.

4. *City of Birmingham vs. Charles Patrick,* 44510-G (Official Report, Recorder's Court, 1954), National Archives, Southeast Region, Case No. 13771; "Board Hears Brutality Case," *Birmingham Mirror,* January 29, 1955; information about Dr. Crayton C. Fargason was provided by ACIPCO communications manager Joy Carter.

5. J. Mills Thornton III, *Dividing Lines: Municipal Politics and the Struggle for Civil Rights in Montgomery, Birmingham and Selma,* (Tuscaloosa: The University of Alabama Press, 2002), 211.

6. "Court Roundup—Parker Is Philosophical as Cases Tried in Court," *Birmingham News*, September 14, 1955.

7. William A. Nunnelley, *Bull Connor* (Tuscaloosa: The University of Alabama Press, 1991), 42.

8. Eskew, *But for Birmingham,* 99; Thornton III, *Dividing Lines,* 181; Report of Citizen's Committee on Birmingham Police Department, February 19, 1952, Reference Department, BPLA, 2.

9. *City of Birmingham vs. Charles Patrick,* 44510-G (Official Report, Recorder's Court, 1954), National Archives, Southeast Region, Case No. 13771.

10. Bill Mobley, "Chief Orders Investigation into Charge that Officer Beat Prisoner," *Birmingham Post-Herald,* December 18, 1954.

11. *City of Birmingham vs. Charles Patrick,* 44510-G, (Official Report, Recorder's Court, 1954), National Archives, Southeast Region, Case No. 13771.

12. Ibid.

13. "Taken Under Advisement—Convicted on Testimony of Fired Pair, Dismissal Asked," *Birmingham News,* December 23, 1954;, "City Commission Votes 30-day Suspension for 2 Policemen," *Birmingham World,* December 31, 1954.

14. "Taken Under Advisement—Convicted on Testimony of Fired Pair, Dismissal Asked," *Birmingham News,* December 23, 1954; "Patrick to Take Lie Test To-

night in Beating Case," *Birmingham News,* January 7, 1955; "Patrick Files Charges Against Two Policemen," *Birmingham World,* January 7, 1955.

15. "Probe Ordered—Man Testifies in Court that Officer Beat Him," *Birmingham News,* December 18, 1954; "Chief Orders Investigation into Charge that Officer Beat Prisoner," *Post-Herald,* December 18, 1954.

16. *City of Birmingham vs. Charles Patrick,* 44510-G (Official Report, Recorder's Court, 1954), National Archives, Southeast Region, Case No. 13771.

17. Ibid.

Chapter 4

1. Thornton III, *Dividing Lines,* 181.

2. Howell Raines quotes from a July 17, 2007, telephone interview with the author.

3. Joe Dickson quotes from February 14, 2004, and March 21, 2008, telephone interviews with the author.

4. "Lindbergh and Pattie Commended by NAACP," *Birmingham World,* January 21, 1955.

5. Eskew, *But for Birmingham,* 99.

6. Thornton III, *Dividing Lines,* 181.

7. Report of Citizen's Committee on Birmingham Police Department, February 19, 1952, 2, Reference Department BPLA.

8. Glenn Alan Feldman, *The Ku Klux Klan in Alabama, 1915–1954,* 460 (UMI Dissertation Services, Auburn University, 1996).

9. "Testimony in Ex-officer's Trial Begins," *Birmingham Post-Herald,* December 7, 1954; "Ex-policeman Is Acquitted of Burglary," *Birmingham Post-Herald,* December 9, 1954; "Jury Declares Dismissed Police Officer Not Guilty," *Birmingham News,* December 9, 1954; "Chief Pattie to File Charges Against Officer J. L. McCain," *Birmingham News,* February 15, 1955.

10. "Officer to Lose Some Off Days in Jailing of Girl," *Birmingham News,* February 18, 1955; "Judges Named for Police Case," *Birmingham Post-Herald,* February 18, 1955; "Firing of Officer Upheld by 3 Judges," *Birmingham Post-Herald,* March 2, 1955; Bill Mobley, "Police Lieutenant Taken Off Force Pending Probe," *Birmingham Post-Herald,* March 15, 1955; "Lt. Jack Warren to Head Police Morning Shift," *Birmingham News,* March 15, 1955.

11. Eskew, *But for Birmingham,* 96; "Fired Officer, Announcer Admit Robbery Attempt," *Birmingham Post-Herald,* October 28, 1953.

12. Harrison E. Salisbury, "Fear and Hatred Grip Birmingham," *New York Times,* April 12, 1960, published in *Reporting Civil Rights, Part One, American Journalism, 1941–1963* (New York: Literary Classics of the United States, Inc., 2003), 450.

13. "Two Policemen Fired in Beating of Prisoner," *Birmingham News,* December 21, 1954; "Two Policemen Fired on Charge of Beating Negro, Assistant Warden at Jail Suspended," *Post-Herald,* December 21, 1954; "Jail-Cell Beating Police Before City Commissioners," *Birmingham World,* December 28, 1954.

14. "Mayor Unlikely to Change Vote in Police Beating," *Birmingham News,* December 30, 1954.

15. "FBI to Probe Charges Officers Beat Prisoner," *Birmingham Post-Herald,* December 21, 1954.

16. "Beaten Prisoner to Press Charges, Lawyer Asked to File State, Federal Counts, Suit Against Two Policemen," *Birmingham Post-Herald,* December 30, 1954.

17. James A. Robey Jr. quotes from a February 28, 2009, telephone interview with the author.

18. "City to Hear Officers Charged in Jail Beating, Police Commissioner Says He Will Offer Resolution Asking Dismissal," *Birmingham Post-Herald,* December 28, 1954.

19. Ibid.

20. The Personnel Board of Jefferson County, Alabama, Minute Book 5, AR. #1944.5.1, 276; "Personnel Board Drops Beating Case Charges, Two Officers Suspended for 30 Days; Action Causes City Commission Split," *Birmingham Post-Herald,* December 29, 1954.

21. "Personnel Board Drops Beating Case Charges, Two Officers Suspended for 30 Days; Action Causes City Commission Split," *Birmingham Post-Herald,* December 29, 1954.

22. "Lindbergh and Morgan Bury Hatchet," *Birmingham Post-Herald,* January 5, 1955.

23. Ibid.

24. Ibid.

25. Eskew, *But for Birmingham,* 104.

26. "Ex-police Captain to Open Law Office," *Birmingham News,* August 21, 1952; "Ex-Capt. Huey Draws New Fine in Speeding Case," *Birmingham News,* October 6, 1952; "Judge Boner Rejects Plea of 'Bud' Huey," *Birmingham Post-Herald,* Sept. 5, 1952. To his credit, C. E. "Bud" Huey earned a law degree while working full-time for the Birmingham Police Department, and Eugene "Bull" Connor had at one time considered him for the next chief of police. His elevation to captain was touted as "the fastest on record since the department was put under the civil service." But misfortune ensued when he admitted before the personnel board in early 1952 to having been arrested in Illinois on a burglary charge as a youth in 1931, a fact he omitted on a civil service questionnaire. Though charges were dropped in 1933, his admission led to a personnel board investigation. He later resigned. "Detective Lt. C. E. Huey Ele-

vated to Rank of Captain," *Birmingham News,* December 4, 1951; "Huey States He Was Freed in Early Case," *Birmingham News,* January 19, 1952.

27. "Personnel Board Drops Beating Case Charges, Two Officers Suspended for 30 Days; Action Causes City Commission Split," *Birmingham Post-Herald,* December 29, 1954.

Chapter 5

1. "Justice?" *Birmingham Post-Herald,* December 29, 1954.

2. John Temple Graves, "This Morning," *Birmingham Post-Herald,* December 30, 1954. In a July 2007 telephone interview with the author, Retired *Post-Herald* reporter Andrew Glaze described John Temple Graves as a "very old-fashioned and conservative" person. Graves was also a descendant of the founders of Wilson Chapel. Alyce Billings Walker, "Historic Wilson Chapel Again Becomes Popular," *Birmingham News,* January 24, 1943.

3. Jerome Cooper, letter to Commissioner Robert E. Lindbergh, December 30, 1954, James W. Morgan Mayoral Papers, File #266.21.23, BPLA. Jerome Cooper, a Harvard Law School graduate and prominent Jewish labor and civil rights attorney, fought for social change in Birmingham throughout his distinguished career. In 1963, he attended President John F. Kennedy's White House meeting that led to the creation of the Lawyers' Committee for Civil Rights Under Law. He once told a reporter, "Only in labor unions was there any common meeting ground of black and white." He retired from his legal practice at the age of ninety and died two months later in October 2003. Jeff Hansen, "Lawyer Jerome Cooper Dies," *Birmingham News,* October 16, 2003; "Obituary: Jerome A. Cooper," *Birmingham News,* October 16, 2003.

4. Mrs. Marlowe Riggins, letter to Mayor Morgan, December 30, 1954, James W. Morgan Mayoral Papers, File #266.21.23, BPLA.

5. "30-day Suspension Is Inadequate in Police Beating of Prisoner," *Birmingham News,* December 29, 1954.

6. "City Should Reconsider Jail Beating Action," *Birmingham News,* January 7, 1955.

7. "Who Struck the Match that Set the House Afire," *Birmingham News,* January 6, 1955; "Agreement With Stand on Police Suspension," *Birmingham News,* January 4, 1955.

8. Anonymous note to Mayor Morgan, January 7, 1955, James W. Morgan Mayoral Papers, File #266.21.24, BPLA.

9. D. Q. Harpless, letter to Mayor Morgan and Commissioner Wade Bradley, December 31, 1954, James W. Morgan Mayoral Papers, File #266.21.23, BPLA.

10. Mae Young, letter to Mayor Morgan, James W. Morgan Mayoral Papers, File #266.21.24, BPLA.

11. Robert H. Loeb, letter to Mayor Morgan, January 27, 1955, James W. Morgan Mayoral Papers, File #266.21.24, BPLA; "Club Raps Beating of Prisoner," *Birmingham News,* January 11, 1955.

12. "Suspension of Policemen in Beating Case Is Attacked," *Birmingham Post-Herald,* January 4, 1955.

13. Ibid.

14. Rufus A. Points, Jr., "Suspension of Policemen Hardly Fits Offense," *Birmingham News,* January 3, 1955; Mrs. J. E. Hall, letter to Mayor Morgan, January 1, 1955, James W. Morgan Mayoral Papers, File #266.21.24, BPLA.

15. "Lindbergh and Morgan Bury Hatchet," *Birmingham Post-Herald,* January 5, 1955.

16. "This Morning," *Birmingham Post-Herald,* January 6, 1955.

17. Resolution of the NAACP Sponsored Mass Meeting, Sixteenth Street Baptist Church, January 16, 1955, James W. Morgan Mayoral Papers, File #266.21.24, BPLA; "Trial Date Set for Policemen Accused of Beating Prisoner," *Birmingham World,* January 14, 1955; "Lindbergh and Pattie Commended by NAACP," *Birmingham World,* January 21, 1955.

18. Arthur Walton quotes are from a July 17, 2006, telephone interview with the author.

19. Joe Dickson quotes are from February 14, 2004, and November 28, 2004, telephone interviews with the author.

20. Thornton III, *Dividing Lines,* 185; "Two Policemen Fired in Beating of Prisoner," *Birmingham News,* December 21, 1954.

21. Dr. Horace Huntley's quotes are from a January 30, 2004, interview with the author at the Birmingham Civil Rights Institute.

22. Ibid.

23. Mrs. J. E. Hall, letter to Mayor Morgan, January 1, 1955, James W. Morgan Mayoral Papers, File #266.21.24, BPLA.

24. Eskew, *But for Birmingham,* 176; Arthur Walton quotes are from a July 17, 2006, telephone interview with the author.

25. Dr. Horace Huntley's quotes are from a January 30, 2004, interview with the author at the Birmingham Civil Rights Institute.

26. "Birmingham jail very nice place," *Birmingham Post-Herald,* January 27, 1955.

27. Anonymous member of Fairview Methodist Church, letter to Commissioners Morgan and Bradley, December 29, 1954, James W. Morgan Mayoral Papers, File #266.21.23, BPLA.

28. Mrs. J. W. Siniard, letter to Mayor Morgan, January 5, 1955, James W. Morgan Mayoral Papers, File #266.21.24, BPLA.

29. Ibid.

30. James "Jim" Baggett's comment about "Bull" Connor teaching Sunday school was noted during a July 2003 conversation with the author at BPLA.

31. Eskew, *But for Birmingham*, 109–13.

32. Galatians 4:19, 5:22–23.

33. Mrs. A. S. Davis, letter to Mayor Morgan, January 5, 1955, James W. Morgan Mayoral Papers, File #266.21.24, BPLA.

34. Glenn Alan Feldman, *The Ku Klux Klan in Alabama, 1915–1954*, (UMI Dissertation Services, Auburn University, 1996), 540. In 1955, Evangelist Dr. Billy Graham echoed Glenn Alan Feldman's sentiment when he told the National Press Club in Washington, D.C., "that anything that makes any person, because of color of his skin, a second-class citizen is not only un-American but it is un-Christian." Dr. Graham went on to say, "I think the church has too long lagged behind . . . and we have allowed other groups to lead in this matter of racial relations." "Billy Graham Hits Churches on Race Stand," *Birmingham World*, August 12, 1955.

35. Feldman, *The Ku Klux Klan in Alabama*, 470; Wyn Craig Wade, *The Fiery Cross: The Ku Klux Klan in America* (New York: Simon and Schuster, Ltd., 1987), 321.

36. Dr. Martin Luther King, Jr., "Letter from Birmingham Jail," April 16, 1963, courtesy of the King Center, Atlanta, Georgia, by way of the Birmingham Civil Rights Institute.

37. Ironically, it would not be the last time the morals of Malcolm L. Wheeler and Officer J. W. Siniard clashed. In 1960, six years after Wheeler presented my father's case, the Alabama Supreme Court heard a case on appeal in which Wheeler represented plaintiff Luther Boykin, a pedestrian, who was injured after a collision between two automobiles driven by Kenneth M. Hayes and Vera B. McCoy. Boykin had initially won a $41,500 judgment against McCoy, but the jury let Hayes off the hook. Boykin therefore moved for a new trial, desiring a judgment against Hayes as well. When the twenty-four prospective jurors were asked during voir dire examination if they were acquainted with "Mr. Parsons or Mr. Malcolm Wheeler, or Mr. Ed Rose of the firm of Parsons, Wheeler and Rose," no one responded. Subsequently, court records noted "that there was a juror who served on said case by the name of James Wendell Siniard who knew Malcolm L. Wheeler . . . but who remained silent and failed or refused to reveal his acquaintance with Malcolm L. Wheeler." Boykin got his new trial. Brutality first placed Siniard in the spotlight. Dishonesty redeployed it. *Kenneth M. Hayes v. Luther Boykin*, 271 Ala. 588, 126 So.2d 91, (July 14, 1960), Jefferson County Law Library, Birmingham, Alabama.

38. James Saxon Childers, "Call of first love too strong to be resisted," Van der Veer, McClellan Papers, File #1051.1.2, BPLA.

39. "News Editor Wins Award for Editorial," *Birmingham News*, February 22,

1959; "Editorial Chief Saw Job: Standing Fast for Right," *Birmingham News,* March 13, 1988.

40. In an August 19, 2003, letter addressed to the author, Virginia Van der Veer Hamilton provided information about her father's career, outlook and writing style, as well as newsroom politics at the *Birmingham News.*

41. Ibid.

42. Ibid.

43. Ibid.

44. Ibid.

45. Ibid.

46. Robert Jensen, *The Heart of Whiteness: Confronting Race, Racism, and White Privilege* (San Francisco: City Lights Publishers, 2005), xx.

Chapter 6

1. "Beaten Prisoner to Press Charges," *Birmingham Post-Herald,* December 30, 1954.

2. "Mayor Unlikely to Change Vote in Police Beating," *Birmingham News,* December 30, 1954.

3. "Lie Test Set for Man in Traffic Wrangle," *Birmingham News,* December 31, 1954.

4. Ibid; "Judge Orders Beaten Man to Take Lie Test," *Birmingham Post-Herald,* December 31, 1954.

5. "Police Chief Says It's Called on Too Frequently—Parker Defends Lie Detector," *Birmingham News,* January 4, 1955.

6. Ibid.

7. Ibid; "To Settle Cases—Police Ask Judge Parker to Stop Using Lie Tests," *Birmingham Post-Herald,* January 4, 1955.

8. "Lie Detectors and Their Use," *Birmingham News,* January 7, 1955.

9. "Second Policeman to Learn Operation," *Birmingham News,* January 4, 1955.

10. Howell Raines quotes from June 26, 2007, e-mail correspondence with the author.

11. Ibid.

12. "Jail Beating Accuser Takes Lie Tests," *Birmingham Post-Herald,* January 8, 1955.

13. "Citizens Here Await Decision on Jail-cell Beating of Negro," *Birmingham World,* January 4, 1955.

14. "City Commission Votes 30-day Suspension for 2 Policemen," *Birmingham World,* December 31, 1954.

15. "Citizens Here Await Decision on Jail-cell Beating of Negro," *Birmingham World*, January 4, 1955.

16. "Board Today May Be Asked to Probe Jail Beating Case," *Birmingham Post-Herald*, January 5, 1955.

17. "Beating Charges Filed Against Two Policemen, Answer Required Within Five Days," *Birmingham Post-Herald*, January 6, 1955; The Personnel Board of Jefferson County, Alabama, Minute Book 5, AR. #1944.5.1, 277, BPLA.

18. Ibid 276–77.

19. "Officers to Get Board Hearing on Jail Beating," *Birmingham News*, January 6, 1955.

20. Ibid.

21. Feldman, *The Ku Klux Klan in Alabama*, 451; Eskew, *But for Birmingham*, 71; Associated Press, "Alabama Remembers Black Soldier's Defiance," *Decatur Daily News*, January 16, 2006, *http://www.decaturdaily.com* (accessed August 15, 2007); Cedric J. Robinson, *Black Movements in America* (Kentucky: Routledge, 1997), 131.

22. "Attorneys Add Further Charges in Beating Case," *Birmingham World*, January 18, 1955.

23. "Being Studied—Results of Patrick Lie Detector Test May Be Known Monday," *Birmingham News*, January 8, 1955.

24. "NAACP Slates Mass Meeting on Jail Beating," *Birmingham World*, January 11, 1955.

25. "Officer Siniard Denies All Accusations in Beating Case," *Birmingham News*, January 12, 1955; "Policemen's Hearing Is Set for January 26," *Birmingham Post-Herald*, January 13, 1955.

26. "Charges Placed Against Jailer in Beating Case," *Birmingham News*, January 13, 1955; "Board Schedules Hearing for Jail Warden," *Birmingham Post-Herald*, January 14, 1955.

27. While my father had said he was not a Mason, he admitted to purchasing a Mason ring, stressing he "didn't go too far."

28. "City Commission Votes 30-day Suspension for 2 Policemen," *Birmingham World*, December 31, 1954.

29. "In Jail Beating Case, Patrick Acquitted of Being Disorderly," *Birmingham Post-Herald*, January 14, 1955.

Chapter 7

1. "Beaten Prisoner to Press Charges," *Birmingham Post-Herald*, December 30, 1954.

2. Howell Raines, *My Soul Is Rested* (New York: G. P. Putnam's Sons, 1977), 348;

Forrest R. White, "Southern States Sidestep Desegregation Orders," in Paul A. Winters, *The Civil Rights Movement,* (San Diego, CA: Greenhaven Press, Inc., 2000), 78; Honorable Earl F. Hilliard, Alabama, U.S. Congressional Record, House of Representatives, February 11, 1997, Arthur Shores Files, Birmingham Civil Rights Institute.

3. Raines, *My Soul Is Rested,* 350–51.

4. Joe Dickson quotes are from a February 14, 2004, telephone interview with the author.

5. Peter Hall Jr. quotes are from a March 2007 interview with the author in Birmingham, Alabama, and a July 2008 e-mail correspondence.

6. Joe Dickson quotes are from a February 14, 2004, telephone interview with the author; Honorable Earl F. Hilliard, Alabama, U.S. Congressional Record, House of Representatives, January 29, 2002, Arthur Shores Files, Birmingham Civil Rights Institute.

7. Comments about Orzell Billingsley Jr. are from a March 2007 interview with a close associate of Malcolm L. Wheeler. In that the interview was conducted in confidentiality, the name has been withheld by mutual agreement. Joe Dickson quote is from a November 28, 2004, telephone interview with the author.

8. Peter Hall Jr. quotes are from a July 2008 e-mail correspondence.

9. Peter Hall Jr. quotes are from a March 2007 interview with the author in Birmingham, Alabama, and a July 2008 e-mail correspondence.

10. Comments about Peter A. Hall Sr. are from a March 2007 interview with a close associate of Malcolm L. Wheeler. In that the interview was conducted in confidentiality, the name has been withheld by mutual agreement.

11. Joe Dickson quotes are from a February 14, 2004, telephone interview with the author.

12. Peter Hall Jr. quotes are from a March 2007 interview with the author in Birmingham, Alabama.

13. *Reeves v. Alabama,* 355 U.S. 368 (1958); *Hamilton v. Alabama,* 368 U.S. 52 (1961); *Fikes v. Alabama,* 352 U.S. 191 (1957); *Shuttlesworth v. Birmingham,* 376 U.S. 339 (1964); Mason Davis comments are from a June 24, 2008, telephone interview with the author.

14. Raines, *My Soul Is Rested,* 348.

15. Nunnelley, *Bull Connor,* 70.

16. "NAACP to Map Installation Plans Thursday Night," *Birmingham World,* January 4, 1955; "Lindbergh and Pattie Commended by NAACP," *Birmingham World,* January 21, 1955.

17. "Officers Suspended in Beating of Prisoner Due on Job This Week," *Birmingham News,* January 16, 1955; "Ex-officer Robert Slaughter Told He'll Lose Probation Plea," *Birmingham News,* January 15, 1955.

18. Sardis Baptist Church letter is from the Charles Patrick scrapbook compiled by Rutha Patrick.

Chapter 8

1. "This Morning," *Birmingham Post-Herald,* January 27, 1955.

2. "Hearings Scheduled in Patrick Case," *Birmingham News,* January 25, 1955.

3. "Public Meeting Issue Debated," *Birmingham News,* January 27, 1955.

4. Ibid.

5. The Personnel Board of Jefferson County, Alabama, Minute Book 5, AR. #1944.5.1, 282, BPLA; "Conflicting Stories Laid to Policemen," *Birmingham Post-Herald,* January 27, 1955; "Testimony Given by Witnesses Corroborates Prisoner's Charges," *Birmingham World,* January 28, 1955.

6. "Conflicting Stories Laid to Policemen," *Birmingham Post-Herald,* January 27, 1955; Marcel Hopson, "Testimony Given by Witnesses Corroborates Prisoner's Charges," *Birmingham World,* January 28, 1955. The newspapers were not in agreement on the exact spellings of witness names. The *Birmingham World* published "Jim Wilson," not "Jim Willman" as published in the *Birmingham News.* And both the *Post-Herald* and the *News* wrote "Jesse Smiley," while the *World* wrote "James Smiley." Personnel board records from 1955 showed "Jesse Smiley" and "Jim Wilmon."

7. Marcel Hopson, "Testimony Given by Witnesses Corroborates Prisoner's Charges," *Birmingham World,* January 28, 1955; "Conflicting Stories Laid to Policemen," *Birmingham Post-Herald,* January 27, 1955; Harry Cook, "Personnel Board Hearing—Two Witnesses Tell of City Jail Beating," *Birmingham News,* January 27, 1955.

8. "Conflicting Stories Laid to Policemen," *Birmingham Post-Herald,* January 27, 1955.

9. Harry Cook, "Personnel Board Hearing—Two Witnesses Tell of City Jail Beating," *Birmingham News,* January 27, 1955.

10. Ibid.

11. Ibid.

12. Ibid.

13. Ibid.

14. Marcel Hopson, "Testimony Given by Witnesses Corroborates Prisoner's Charges," *Birmingham World,* January 28, 1955; Alford Stone, "Board Hears Brutality Case," *Birmingham Mirror,* January 29, 1955. According to James Baggett, head of the Department of Manuscripts and Archives at BPLA, Alford Stone was the managing editor of the *Birmingham Mirror.*

15. The Personnel Board of Jefferson County, Alabama, Minute Book 5, AR. #1944.5.1, 281, 284, BPLA.

16. "Decision Near on Jail Beating Laid to Officers," *Birmingham News,* January 28, 2955; "Board Postpones Beating Decision, Motion to Throw Out Case Overruled," *Birmingham Post-Herald,* January 28, 1955.

17. Ibid.

18. Ibid.

19. Ibid.

20. Ibid.

21. "Board Postpones Beating Decision," *Birmingham Post-Herald,* January 28, 1955.

22. The Personnel Board of Jefferson County, Alabama, Minute Book 5, AR. #1944.5.1, 285, BPLA; Andrew Glaze Jr., "Chief Reclaims Badges—Two 'Beating Case' Policemen Fired," *Birmingham Post-Herald,* January 29, 1955; "On Order of Personnel Board—Two Policemen Are Fired for Beating Negro Prisoner in Jail," *Birmingham News,* January 29, 1955; "Policemen Lynch & Siniard Dismissed from Force," *Birmingham World,* February 1, 1955.

23. "Policemen Lynch & Siniard Dismissed from Force," *Birmingham World,* February 1, 1955.

24. The Personnel Board of Jefferson County, Alabama, Minute Book 5, AR. #1944.5.1, 285, BPLA; Opinion and Decision, Personnel Board of Jefferson County, Alabama, *Charles Patrick vs. A.S. Lynch Jr., J. W. Siniard and Earl J. Jackson,* January 28, 1955, BPLA.

25. "Siniard Ineligible to Be Policeman Here Again," *Birmingham News,* February 1, 1955.

26. "Policemen Lynch & Siniard Dismissed From Police Force," *Birmingham World,* February 1, 1955.

27. "Two City Commissioners Absent, Meeting Off," *Birmingham News,* February 1, 1955.

28. "Police Divisions Get New Leaders," *Birmingham Post-Herald,* January 29, 1955; "Police Minimum Age Raised From 20 to 23," *Birmingham Post-Herald,* February 10, 1955.

29. "Exams For Police Jobs to be March 1," *Birmingham News,* February 15, 1955; "City May Hire Policewomen, Says Morgan," *Birmingham Post-Herald,* February 16, 1955.

30. See Chapter 4, notes 9–11.

31. "Pattie Holding Private Talks With Officers," *Birmingham Post-Herald,* March 8, 1955.

32. "Ex-Policeman Sues for $100,000 Claiming He Lost Job Due to NAACP," *Birmingham Post-Herald,* September 24, 1955; "Ex-Policeman Lynch Files Notice of Appeal," *Birmingham News,* February 4, 1955; "Ex-officer Files $100,000 Suit Against NAACP," *Birmingham News,* September 24, 1955; "NAACP, Officers, Mem-

bers Face $100,000 Suit Here," *Birmingham World,* September 27, 1955; "People, Places and Things," *Chicago Defender,* October 8, 1955, national edition, http://www .proquest.com.catalog.houstonlibrary.org/ (accessed September 16, 2009).

33. "To File Charges Against Ex-officers in Beating Case," *Birmingham World,* February 11, 1955.

34. Andrew Glaze Jr., "Chief Reclaims Badges—Two 'Beating Case' Policemen Fired," *Birmingham Post-Herald,* January 29, 1955; "On Order of Personnel Board— Two Policemen Are Fired for Beating Negro Prisoner in Jail," *Birmingham News,* January 29, 1955.

Chapter 9

1. *United States v. Arthur Steven Lynch Jr., James Wendell Siniard, Earl James Jackson,* 18 U.S.C. 242 (1955); "Three Indicted in Jail Cell Beating of City Prisoner," *Birmingham News,* February 24, 1955; Edward Pilley, "Ex-Policemen and Warden—3 Indicted by U.S. in Beating at Jail," *Birmingham Post-Herald,* February 24, 1955; "3 Indicted in Connection With Jail-Cell Beating Case," *Birmingham World,* February 25, 1955.

2. *United States v. Arthur Steven Lynch Jr., James Wendell Siniard, Earl James Jackson,* 18 U.S.C. 242 (1955); Edward Pilley, "Ex-Policemen and Warden—3 Indicted by U.S. in Beating at Jail," *Birmingham Post-Herald,* February 24, 1955.

3. Mason Davis quotes are from a September 5, 2003, telephone interview with the author; "Tops in Our Town," *Birmingham News,* September 26, 1957.

4. "Federal Court Jury Organized in Civil Rights Case," *Birmingham News,* June 1, 1955.

5. Don Cummins, "Three Are Acquitted in Civil Rights Case," *Birmingham Post-Herald,* June 3, 1955.

6. Alice Gardner Murphy, "Civil Rights Trial Over Jail Beating Is Nearing Jury," *Birmingham News,* June 2, 1955.

7. Alice Gardner Murphy, "Ex-policemen Freed in Federal Civil Rights Case," *Birmingham News,* June 3, 1955.

8. Edward Pilley, "Government Rests Case in Civil Rights Trial," *Birmingham Post-Herald,* June 2, 1955.

9. "Federal Court Jury Organized in Civil Rights Case," *Birmingham News,* June 1, 1955; Mason Davis's comments were from an August 2007 telephone interview with the author.

10. *United States v. Arthur Steven Lynch Jr., James Wendell Siniard, Earl James Jackson,* 18 U.S.C. 242 (1955); Don Cummins, "Three Are Acquitted in Civil Rights Case," *Birmingham Post-Herald,* June 3, 1955; "Tops in Our Town," *Birmingham News,* September 26, 1957.

11. *United States v. Arthur Steven Lynch Jr., James Wendell Siniard, Earl James Jackson,* 18 U.S.C. 242 (1955).

12. Alice Gardner Murphy, "Ex-Policemen Freed in Federal Civil Rights Case," *Birmingham News,* June 3, 1955.

13. Alice Gardner Murphy, "Civil Rights Trial Over Jail Beating Is Nearing Jury," *Birmingham News,* June 2, 1955.

14. Alice Gardner Murphy, "Ex-Policemen Freed in Federal Civil Rights Case," *Birmingham News,* June 3, 1955.

15. Ibid; "3 Alabama Cops Who Beat Negro, Freed," *Chicago Defender,* June 25, 1955, national edition, http://www.proquest.com.catalog.houstonlibrary.org/ (accessed September 16, 2009).

16. Eskew, *But for Birmingham,* 135; Thornton III, *Dividing Lines,* 207, 218, 225.

17. Jack Bass, *Unlikely Heroes* (Tuscaloosa and London: The University of Alabama Press, 1981), 67–69.

18. James A. Robey Jr. comments are from a February 28, 2009, telephone interview with the author; "FBI Announces Police School on Civil Rights," *Birmingham Post-Herald,* February 22, 1956; "Policemen Hear of Civil Rights," *Birmingham Post-Herald,* February 24, 1956.

19. Alice Gardner Murphy, "Ex-Policemen Freed in Federal Civil Rights Case," *Birmingham News,* June 3, 1955.

20. Don Cummins, "Three Are Acquitted in Civil Rights Case," *Birmingham Post-Herald,* June 3, 1955.

21. *Report of Citizens' Committee on Birmingham Police Department,* February 19, 1952, (BPL Reference Department), 9; Feldman, *The Ku Klux Klan in Alabama, 1915–1954,* 471.

22. Eskew, *But for Birmingham,* 67–68; Andrew M. Manis, *A Fire You Can't Put Out: The Civil Rights Life of Birmingham's Reverend Fred Shuttlesworth* (Tuscaloosa: The University of Alabama Press, 1999), 80; Howell Raines quotes are from June 26, 2007, e-mail correspondence with the author.

23. "3-Judge Panel Upholds Firing of Policeman," *Birmingham World,* July 5, 1955.

Chapter 10

1. Jensen, *Heart of Whiteness,* 2–3.

2. Paul A. Winters, *The Civil Rights Movement* (San Diego, CA: Greenhaven Press, Inc., 2000), 15.

3. Quoted in Nunnelley, *Bull Connor,* 5.

4. Jensen, *Heart of Whiteness,* xx.

5. Eskew, *But for Birmingham,* 118–19. Commissioner Lindbergh lost the 1957 commissioner's race to Connor by 103 votes.

6. Comments about Eugene "Bull" Connor are from a July 15, 2003, telephone interview with a close associate of Malcolm L. Wheeler. In that the interview was conducted in confidentiality, the name has been withheld by mutual agreement.

7. *Report of Citizen's Committee on Birmingham Police Department,* February 19, 1952, 11.

8. "Negro Police Not Needed, Says Connor, Asserts He Never Will Appoint Them," *Birmingham Post-Herald,* February 11, 1953; *Report of Citizen's Committee on Birmingham Police Department,* February 19, 1952, 2.

9. Manis, *A Fire You Can't Put Out,* 82.

10. "Lindbergh and Pattie Commended by NAACP," *Birmingham World,* January 21, 1955; Eskew, *But for Birmingham,* 104.

11. Manis, *A Fire You Can't Put Out,* 81.

12. "Mayor, Other City Leaders, in Favor of Adding Negroes to Force," *Birmingham World,* June 24, 1955; "Spokesman for Ministers Wants Race Policemen," *Birmingham World,* July 29, 1955; "City May Hire Policewomen, Says Morgan," *Birmingham Post-Herald,* February 16, 1955.

13. Ed Stack letter to city commission, Young Men's Business Club, August 1, 1955, James W. Morgan Mayoral Papers, File #266.18.35, BPLA; Eskew, *But for Birmingham,* 124; Manis, *A Fire You Can't Put,* 84. Manis wrote that seventy-six ministers signed Shuttlesworth's petition, while Eskew wrote that seventy-seven did.

14. Eskew, *But for Birmingham,* 124.

15. Ibid., 15–17, 124–27.

16. Ibid., 118–19.

17. Ibid., 4.

18. Raines, *My Soul Is Rested,* 155.

19. Eskew, *But for Birmingham,* 4, 338.

20. Raines, *My Soul Is Rested,* 161.

21. John Hurst, "Civil Rights Movement Origins at Highlander Educational Sessions," *Race, Poverty & the Environment* 14, no. 2 (Fall 2007); Kathy Emery and Eric Mar, "Democratizing the Public School System," *Race, Poverty & the Environment,* 14, no. 2 (Fall 2007); Eliot Wigginton, *Refuse to Stand Silently By: An Oral History of Grass Roots Social Activism in America, 1921–1964* (New York: Doubleday, 1992), xvii, 231.

22. Wigginton, *Refuse to Stand Silently,* 232.

23. Ibid., 234.

24. Eskew, *But for Birmingham,* iv.

Epilogue

1. *Ungawa!* was Tarzan's authoritative roar in Hollywood's popular "jungle fantasies." Later, it was paired with "Black power!" and became a chant adopted by Cali-

fornia youth during the Black Power Movement. Mwalimu J. Shujaa, "The widening gap between education and schooling in the post 9/11 era," *The Journal of Negro Education*, 72:2 (Spring 2003): 179; Frederica Mathewes-Green, "Ungawa! The curiously compelling saga of Tarzan," *Christianity Today*, September 1, 2005, http://www.ctlibrary.com/bc/2005/sepoct/9.23.html (accessed September 16, 2009).

2. Robert J. Norrell, *The House I Live In: Race in the American Century* (New York: Oxford University Press, 2005), 186, 232.

3. Ibid., 232–33.

4. Ibid., 233.

Index

Page numbers in italics refer to figures.